WORKPLACE COMMUNICATION

Communicating is More Than Message Distribution

Internal & External Practices Ready for Implementation

© 2014 KENNY BARKLEY. All Rights reserved
ISBN 978-1-312-12724-1

AUTHOR AND PUBLISHER:
Kenny Barkley

EDITOR:
Debbie McArdle

All rights reserved. No part of this publication may be reproduced, distributed, or transmitted in any form or by any means, including photocopying, recording, or other electronic or mechanical methods, without the prior written permission of the publisher, except in the case of brief quotations embodied in critical reviews and certain other noncommercial uses permitted by copyright law.

TABLE OF CONTENTS

Chapter 1
THE COMMUNICATOR
The Lifeblood of Every Business
Communication Skills: You Have Them!
Communicator's Role as Town Crier

Chapter 2
KNOWING YOUR TARGET AUDIENCE
Who is Your Target Audience?
Building Blocks for Creating a Message
Pantry Test – Writing for the Masses
Hierarchical Messaging
Let's Be Transparent

Chapter 3
INTERNAL COMMUNICATION PRACTICES
Internal Communication: It's the Bomb!
Making a Communication Evolution Model
State of the Business Address
A Succinct PowerPoint Presentation
Communicating During Layoffs
Communicating a Company Acquisition
Make Email Work for You
Building & Maintaining an Intranet Site
Teach Business Basics to Your Employees
Telephones: Setting Up an Info Line
Lunch and Learn
Meetings – the Necessary Evil
Addressing Workplace Rumors

Publishing an Employee Photo Calendar

Chapter 4
DESKTOP PUBLISHING
Establishing Your Desktop System
Creating Newsletters

Chapter 5
COMMUNICATING FOR RESULTS
Making Communication Work for You
Creating a High-Level Roadmap
Identifying and Mapping Stakeholders
High-Level Communications Calendar
Key Performance Indicators & Dashboards

Chapter 6
PROMOTING SAFETY THROUGH COMMUNICATION
Safety: It's Everybody's Business
Designing Safety Posters
Motivate Employees Through the BRAVO! Program
Building a Crisis Communication Plan
Emergency Quick Reference Guide
Other Safety Communication Ideas

Chapter 7
EXTERNAL COMMUNICATION PRACTICES
Employees are Public Relations Activists
Giving Credit to Get Credit
Contributing to Non-Profit Groups
Annual Community Report
Something for the Kids: A Coloring Book
Establishing an Internet Site

Starting a Visitor Ambassador Program
Write Speeches to Inform
Public Surveys Can Be Useful – But Beware

Chapter 8
WORKING WITH JOURNALISTS
Building Relationships with Journalists
Everything is on the Record
Writing Press Releases
Creating a Q & A List

Chapter 9
EMPLOYEE INCENTIVE PROGRAMS
Giving Back to Your Employees
Implementing a Club 100 Program
Establishing a First Snow Contest
Organizing Company Picnics

Chapter 10
EMPLOYEE FEEDBACK
Putting Together a Q&A Forum
Incorporating Employee Surveys

About the Author

Kenny Barkley entered the communication field as he emerged from his mother's womb. Within seconds after being born, the doctor slapped his butt, causing the toddler to let out a penetrating noise. Mom, Dad, and the medical staff knew he'd invaded the world. Since that day, he has continued communicating for the last 50 years, shrilling through more understandable methods such as reading, writing, designing, and marketing.

At the tender age of fifteen, Kenny stepped into the communication field as a member of his high school yearbook and newsletter staffs. In addition, he also volunteered as a disc jockey at friends' parties. One year later, he moved to Florida where he enrolled in a broadcasting school in hopes of carving out a career in radio.

He graduated from the broadcasting school and moved back home, where he started college classes, majoring in communication. A decent student, Kenny joined the college newspaper staff as a reporter and advertising sales. He also attended radio and television classes, believing it would lead him to a job. The following year, he moved away from sales and took on a disc jockey position at a local radio station.

He eventually received a bachelor's degree in journalism and a master's in mass communication and spent several years in radio, newspaper, internal and external communication, and corporate communication. Over the years, Kenny won several state newspaper writing and photography awards and received national magazine recognition for a screenplay treatment. His photographs have appeared in several books and magazines; he researched, wrote and published a community sustainability report; and he co-authored the book <u>School-to-Work: Kentucky's Best Practices</u>. Kenny also taught adult computer classes and business classes. He's currently working on a novel, intermingling comedy and philosophy.

Dedication

To my wife, Janet, and my two boys, Aaron and Logan – both of whom are creeping toward a career in communication. "Come on in, boys. The water is fine!"

Acknowledgements

You know, there are few new ideas in this world. Many of us take what somebody else accomplished in the past and then mutate his or her work to fit our needs. I didn't invent photography, writing, marketing, design; I just utilize what I've learned over the years – what I've been taught and experienced during my career.

I am inspired by communication and the people who use it to improve the quality of life. So, let me acknowledge and say thanks to everyone who has provided me with tips on incorporating high-quality communication practices.

Introduction

For several years, I've had the urge to write a book on communication practices. After working directly with non-profit and for-profit organizations for over twenty-five years, I've learned they have one thing in common – the need for effective communication.

The key word is "effective."

During my career, which I hope is far from over, I've evaluated and observed a bounty of constructive communication practices and managed to generate a few of my own, particularly in the internal and external realms and in employee relations. Just as important, I've witnessed poor communication applications and strategies which precipitated damage to organizations.

I am a communication practitioner, not a scholar. While I don't qualify academically as a scholar or social scientist, I do have a Master's degree in mass communication. I enjoyed the values of my collegiate experience and the associated academic research, but theories or philosophical discussions didn't lead me to a successful communication career – it continues to be the actual practices.

What I learned over the course of my career is many communication consultants, communication related books, magazine articles, periodical columns, and web sites find difficulty in getting to the point. Even worse, they rarely offer organizations' effective communication techniques. They are proficient in conveying theories and explanations, which is great reading material if the time is available, but my inclination is to skip the formalities and jump into the water, head first. Provide me the tools and ideas, man. Throw me a bone.

What we pine for nowadays is for someone to confer upon communicators and companies some useful ideas and the steps to follow for implementing them.

My aspiration is to offer you advice in relation to communication crafts and tangible practices – and the steps to implement them. With these tools, communication can make a tremendous impact on your organization. I don't claim to be the best communicator, just one who believes in the nuts and bolts. I wish to provide people with something they can use.

I am a communication fundamentalist by heart, an atypical characteristic swamped by the over-electrifying and self-indulgent practices coveted by the younger generation. People want to sidestep the practicalities and go straight for the summit without building a foundation to support their long-term objectives. I believe this is a mistake.

Generally speaking, people desire to do the fun stuff and pass along the hard work to someone else. It's like my wife and I painting a room in our house. She wants to do the walls, and leave me with the trim job. She likes to wash the car but wants me to clean the windows. It doesn't take a scholar to figure out why. Painting the walls and washing the car provides immediate, gratifying results. Those of us stuck with painting around the light switch or cleaning the windows don't get much out of it – it's a necessary evil and not the least bit sexy.

I want you to understand how communication can improve business planning and also boost the probability your organization will accomplish its goals. Proficient communication – and inferior communication – takes hard work. It is more than sending out an email to all employees. It's about encouraging employees to take a personal stake in the business. It isn't easy, folks, but it is doable.

Communication is vital.

Have you ever noticed how television sports reporters tend to use a plethora of clichés to describe particular plays? Sometimes it happens so frequently you can often guess what they're about to say. Another quirk sport reporters have is comparing athletes. They're rather irresolute regarding their comparisons and tend not to stick their necks out too far. As an example, sports pundits declare a certain athlete or game is *"ONE* of the best" in history. They purposely avoid saying "the best" or "the worst" because they're afraid to take responsibility for their assessment. You see, saying "*ONE* of the best" leaves some wiggle room just in case they can be proven wrong.

Unlike these sports reporters, here is one comment that you can take to the bank: Communication is the MOST important business tool in the world! There are no ifs, ands or buts about it.

My first argument: take a minute and visualize what business would be like without communication – no conversations, no writing, no presentations, no flailing of arms…nothing. Now, figure out a way to explain your visualizations to someone without using any of these verbal, written or visual methods. Guess what? Nothing would happen. We'd all be sitting around like a bunch of stumps.

If you want to meet a friend at the golf course, then how do you plan it? What if something ails you, how can you explain it to the doctor? Want to articulate the need for better sales at your business, how will it be accomplished? How will you disagree with this contention put before you?

This isn't a simplistic argument with reference to the importance of communication, but rather a self-evident fact that you can't effectively move through life without it; therefore, why not find a way to perfect it in the workplace? Communication is the foundation in which all for-profit and non-profit organizations operate. Granted there are thousands of tools to make us more efficient, but they can't hold a light to efficient communication.

COMMUNICATION PRACTICES ANYONE CAN USE

Speaking of my wife, she is also skillful at something else. She is a magnificent yard sale (or garage sale) person. She learned the trade from the best, which was my mother, who, rest her soul, was the consummate yard sale professional. Every Thursday when the newspaper listed the weekend's yard sales, my mother would analyze them with great circumspect and then assemble a map for the most efficient route. She wouldn't crisscross; she didn't have the time. Like me, she was a practitioner of her passion – she knew how to "yard sale" through experiences and by trial and error.

People with considerable experience in the yard sale trade – particularly the buyers – are quite ingenious at their trade and know where, when and how to capture the best deals. The more affluent neighborhoods are usually among the first to get called upon because "yard-sellers" tend to speculate wealthier people sell their stuff for less money – not because they need the money. They figure the wealthier people want to rid themselves of clothes and trinkets to make room for newer items. Additionally, wealthier people tend to purchase more brand-named merchandise. Thus, the perception is better bargains can be found at higher class yard sales.

My mom didn't need a Ph.D to figure out that one, just experience, which she shared with my wife.

When my wife and I first married, I had a newspaper reporter's position paying less than $7 an hour; her job earned nine bucks an hour. We weren't poor, and we didn't spend beyond our means; certainly we were not affluent. But we were smart, particularly my wife. She didn't mind purchasing second-hand objects as long as they were of reasonable quality.

One Saturday during our first year of marriage, my mother invited my wife to go "yard- selling" with her. She gladly accepted the offer, while I remained home painting the bathroom trim. They left at 5 a.m., and by noon she drove home with a car full of stuff – a few things we still own after 25-plus years of marriage. Actually, the dining room table we use now was purchased during her first garage sale adventure.

Year in and year out, those two would make the weekly trip around the city to attend yard sales. When my mother passed away 10 years later, my wife continued the yard sale tradition. She doesn't go as often anymore, but she still enjoys them, especially in the summer. Most of the time, she goes not knowing what she will find, but she goes anyway just for the thrill of the catch and the opportunity to find a sweet deal on something we don't need.

Personally, I prefer to go shopping when I fancy something in particular. But sometimes, curious fellows like me get a kick out of rummaging through other people's belongings with no commitment to buy.

One fine summer morning, I trekked along with my wife to some yard sales with the hope of finding a used messenger bag – an old-fashioned leather bag having the appearance of being used for many years. From 6-9 a.m., we trudged along with no luck. There were several satchel bags and messenger bags, but not what I wanted.

I joined her again the following weekend still intent on finding the bag I wanted. To my good fortune, I found exactly what I was looking for – and it was only $3. So, I bought it and continue to use it.

So where does the yard sale scenario fit in with this book? As I began writing, I struggled over how to format the book. I wanted it to help readers, offering easy-to-use templates on communication practices that I've used over and over with great success. With that in mind, and knowing business communicators don't have a lot of time to "crisscross" – so to speak – I chose to write this book with minimal fluff, but with some great ideas at bargain prices.

So, consider me your "yard sale" communication consultant. Within these pages, you shall discover some advantageous practices, not high-priced ideas hawked by a highly paid consultant.

I will not expand to any great extent on subjects or ideas – instead, I'll give them to you with some expectation that you will be clever enough to tailor these ideas to your needs. I came from a journalism background, so I clearly understand the requisite for getting to the point – which I hope you will appreciate. Furthermore, I have used every tool, technique or messaging system that is listed in the book; otherwise, I would have left it out.

Like my mom, I'll provide you with some directions and how to receive the biggest bang for your buck. But, most of all, I will present you with suggestions on how to construct something tangible. Heck, I'll even throw myself under the bus by telling you about some of my failed efforts. My goal is to offer you something for your dollar – a product you can initiate and use, not just advice on how to make communication better. I can search the internet and find advice and theory on the best way to communicate, and I know you can do the same. You want something to hold, to be proud of, and to be relevant for your business or organization.

So, for all of you bargain hunters, continue on.

The Communicator

Every person is a communicator, right?

Chapter 1

THE LIFEBLOOD OF EVERY BUSINESS

Communicators are the backbone to any business – and that's not just referring to professional communicators who possess university degrees and/or 25 years of related experience. Everyone is a communicator. Albeit there are some who have incredible skills to advance their respective organization, while others can cause theirs to sink into the depths of disarray with just a simple internal memo.

There are numerous types of communicators, too. Some excel in the written word, while others enjoy the gift of gab. Some are terrific at creating the message, while others are proficient in disseminating it. We can usually spot talented communicators when we hear or see their work because they project an aura of competence and the distinct ability to articulate their message. One such communicator was Walter Cronkite. He had voice of credibility to put us at ease or persuade us to get off the couch and do something in reaction.

Another fine communicator was Paul Harvey, a radio personality who crafted his news reporting and commentary to resemble a personal conversation. He talked to you, not at you. Mr. Harvey did not resort to loud, crass or obligatory speech to get his point across. Hearing his signature voice was as soothing as it was distinctive.

From the job perspective, there are a number of careers in the communication field, most notably journalism, marketing, and public relations. However, if you're proficient in one of these areas, you can be accomplished in them all with concentration and effort.

If you are fortunate to work in a company employing a communication staff, then you will find each person tends to migrate toward his or her stronger areas of interest. However, if *YOU* are the communication staff at your business, then expect to do a little bit of it all. And it isn't an adverse circumstance, either – being considered a jack of all trades. One day you are writing a newsletter and the next standing in front of television cameras defending your organization.

Of course, there are also downsides to working as a business communicator. Communication professionals are easy targets when projects don't go as planned. How many times have we heard, "It was a miscommunication," or "No one told me about it." Those excuses are the battle cries from colleagues not wanting to take responsibility for their own communication shortcomings. Actually, the communication profession takes a huge amount of blame – often serving as a scapegoat for poor performance.

But the biggest problem with communication in the workplace is when senior management habitually underestimates the profession's potential. They often consider communication to be nothing more than a soft skill worthy only of a passing gesture. In fact, if there were 10 staff people lined up against the wall, and one of them was being forced out, the communication person would likely be in the top three.

Communicators are duty-bound to prove themselves and the value of their field. A communication professional who doesn't take it upon herself to be part of the solution can be profiled and devalued by management if she is only expected to provide an outlet for disseminating news. Communicators must apply their skills to help a business improve, and they can accomplish this with some vision, creativity and practice. Thus, the best avenue one can take for incorporating a reliable communication ecosystem is to perfect the fundamentals.

COMMUNICATION SKILLS: YOU HAVE THEM!

When you get the chance, take a look at the "Employment" section of a Sunday newspaper and carefully examine available jobs at local companies. Pay specific attention to the positions surrounded by black border, because they tend to be aimed at recruiting professionals.

Usually toward the end of the classified advertisement, and as part of the job description, you will see many positions that require "good communication skills." When prospective applicants see this, it's likely nine out of ten presume they meet this requirement. And, why would they not? They're able to talk, listen, understand, and write. Thus, they boast acceptable communication skills, right? Unless they've lost a job due to poor communication performance, they assume there's nothing wrong with their skills.

It's not until a face-to-face interview that you'll discover whether they encompass the communication skills desired. I recall one such interview where our company was hiring an engineer and a particular candidate only answered "yes" or "no" to each question – without enthusiasm, I might add. No kidding – "yes" or "no". But, this guy thought he had compelling communication skills. On the other end of the scale, there are some candidates who don't know when to shut up. It happens more often than the former example but is no more interesting.

Having communication skills is one thing; using them effectively is another.

So, what are "good" communication skills? It's a loaded question, indeed, and could be answered one hundred different ways. But, here are some credentials offered by human resource professionals, and consultants. (Please note that this list is developed through discussions with human resource professionals.)

- Talk properly
- Listen attentively
- Excellent reading skills
- Know how to search for information
- Properly codify records
- Judge someone's "chemistry"

- Take good photographs
- Demonstrate exceptional presentation skills
- Know how to use photographs, even if you did not take them
- Paint a picture with words
- Write a story or memo
- Create a newsletter
- Know how to say 'no'
- Delegate with tact
- Properly respond to criticism
- Use body language
- Write speeches
- Demonstrate adequate public speaking skills
- Know when to speak
- Know when to be quiet
- To compliment others
- Provide negative feedback with elegance
- Facilitate meetings
- Understand responses from others
- Reach agreements or consensus
- Agree without being disagreeable
- Have a wide vocabulary
- Manage your emotions
- Know when to ask for help and to never give up
- Mutually solve problems
- Display proper manners
- Use the "I" word to express feelings
- Be a positive thinker
- Provide visual clues
- Avoid confusing and ambiguous language
- Have patience
- Deliver consistent messages
- Demonstrate enthusiasm in your work

- Know your subject (this skill is commonly abused)
- Know how to write grants
- Exhibit excellent research capabilities
- Understand different cultures
- Implement conflict resolution practices
- Able to build bridges
- Know when to lie
- Know how to motivate
- Able to use several computer programs
- Able to communicate when people leave you speechless
- Create trust between co-workers
- Express opinions and insight on a safe environment
- Share information between colleagues
- Develop unity towards a common goal.

Not to appear facetious, but as one can see by this list of qualifications, the quality of a person's communication skills depends on what someone else considers "good." Keep in mind, though, no one has perfected all of these skills, so don't knock yourself if conflict resolution isn't your cup of tea. There are some people who can develop a PowerPoint presentation capable of triggering a reaction from the salivary glands, but they can't present it to people because they haven't refined those presentation skills.

Many of the skills just listed can be taught in a classroom; others require natural ability like listening skills. Using sports as an example, a professional basketball team would clamor at the chance to transform a 7'3" guy into a starting center, even though he never played basketball. It's a guarantee they can teach him how to rebound, shoot a free throw, learn a hook shot, and dunk a ball. Having the choice between a 5'5" guy who already knows how to play basketball and the tall guy, you can bet a majority of teams would rather sign the 7'3" project instead. You can't teach height.

The point is: everyone has communication skills. However, knowing how and when to incorporate them – vis-à-vis, effective usage – is the objective of proficient communication.

COMMUNICATOR'S ROLE AS THE TOWN CRIER

"Don't blame me; I'm just the messenger." You've heard it before – the retort from the person carrying dreadful news to the masses. No one likes to be the harbinger of difficult news, but somebody's got to do it, right? As the communicator, this reasonability is yours, unless the message is serious enough to be conveyed by the top manager or business owner.

Handling and announcing upsetting news requires talent, especially if a covey of reporters are standing in front of you waiting to hear the company's explanation about an industrial accident. It is a most intimidating moment for a business communicator – facing the possibility of saying the wrong thing to the press and then witness it backfire on the company.

As the stalwart communicator, you are embracing an immense responsibility to propagate accurate messages. If you are incorrect because of careless mistakes, then you begin to punch holes in your credibility. Career ending, fatal inaccuracies rarely occur, but the damage caused by delivering an improper message can be long lasting.

I put myself in one of those situations a few years ago during our company's collective bargaining agreement negotiations. In addition to serving on the negotiation's team, I was also the spokesperson during the month-long negotiations' process. It was a marginally benign position to be in since our policy was to refuse media interviews during negotiations or, at the least, be very nebulous as to what was occurring. The union didn't incorporate the same behavior and would talk if a microphone was positioned in front of them.

One of the company's key sticking points was to change or eliminate the attendance policy because it was feeble and rather generous to those who wanted to miss work. After debating and eventually agreeing on the subject early in the negotiations, we put the issue to bed.

At the end of negotiations, I made myself available to a television news crew who had been waiting in the foyer for four hours. When the tape began rolling, I was asked a number of questions, including our sticking points of which I noted employee attendance was a major problem. I went a step further, rightly or wrongly, and said employees need to attend work and quit using personal days to take off – they were hired because we needed them.

Sounds reasonable and a prudent course of action, right? Instead of directly telling employees our position, I chose to use the television news as my soundboard. I knew full well that my target audience, the employees, would be watching the news so I figured a message concerning attendance would help our cause.

However, my political wrangling didn't set well with the union workforce. In fact, my comments sounded a bit condescending after I heard them, which was part of the reason why there was a backlash over the next three days. While my polarizing comments to the media didn't result in any long-term damage, I learned my lesson in relation to scolding workers through the media. I thought since I was the town crier, I retained the right to set the agenda.

Another challenging aspect for the town crier is he or she might be expected to put into plain words information about subject matter they are not familiar with. People can smell ineptitude from a mile away, so if it requires you to fake it, make sure you at least know the essentials. It might require a crash course in safety – no pun intended – if you are addressing a safety or security concern. Granted, it isn't necessary to be aware of everything, but you need to be able to speak of a subject with some intellect.

Knowing Your Target Audience

Developing the Message

Chapter 2

WHO IS YOUR TARGET AUDIENCE?

This particular subject, Knowing Your Target Audience, is the most critical component in creating an effective and sustainable communication system. If you were to ask me who the target audience is for this book, I would say it's the business communicator – someone who is responsible for any communication aspect at his or her workplace. If you match this description, then you are my target audience. If you are a lab technician at a hospital, I love you, but this book is not geared toward your profession. You could probably use some of the work I've done, but this probably isn't your idea of professional development.

By description, a target audience includes people who you determine have an interest in your message or product. The key words there are, "who you determine" to be the audience of choice. However, business communicators most often don't get to choose their target audience; instead they have to learn to communicate to an audience already given to them – like a mixture of co-workers on the assembly line, financial professionals, managers, maintenance guys and IT folks.

Knowing your target audience signifies you are familiar with the people you are communicating to – you understand the correct balance of literacy and explanation to form logical messages acceptable to a particular person or group of people. It doesn't claim they will like the message; they just need to understand it.

For example, if you are accountable for preparing communication for a company CEO or other executive who has to come across smart to shareholders, then it's okay – to an extent – to be a bit overindulgent in the complexity of your messages. But if you are sending the same message to a group of guys on an assembly line, you better get to the point a bit faster because they don't have the option of sitting in a board room and listening to ongoing discussions.

A college professor in a screenwriting class I once attended gave me some helpful advice regarding how to write for a particular audience: he suggested that when we write a script, think about the movie star playing the lead role. If writing a gangster movie, think of Robert DeNiro; if writing a comedy, think of Jim Carrey.

In workplace terminology, if you are thinking of the CEO when you are writing an employee newsletter, you will write for the CEO. If you are creating a PowerPoint presentation for a production line crew and you are thinking of the plant manager, guess who's your target audience? At the same time, it isn't insinuating that you are obliged to "dumb down" your content; it means you communicate to serve your customers.

Peppered throughout this book will be constant reminders that you must know your target audience before moving on with a communication project. Please keep this in the back of your mind at all times.

BUILDING BLOCKS FOR CREATING A MESSAGE

You've probably heard the old saying, "A picture is worth a thousand words." That simply means when a person looks upon a picture, his or her interpretation of that image may be endless. Thus, it's not necessarily the photo that tells the story but what is happening in the photo and the viewer's imagination.

Yet, if someone told you, "One word is worth a thousand pictures", how would you convey that meaning? If you were to look upon the word "dog", your subconscious fills your brain with memory and images of various dogs.

So, if one word is this powerful, imagine what a writer can do with a hundred.

A principal point to remember about creating a message or constructing a news article is to give customers (readers) enough information so they understand what's going on. That may be an understatement, but it's easier said than done. Writers should incorporate the 5Ws and H into their message: "Who" is the subject is; "What" it's about; "Where" it's happening; "When" it's occurring; "Why" it's happening; and, if appropriate, "How" it happened. This is what aspiring reporters first learn in journalism school – the building blocks of a news story.

Next, reporters will write stories based on the inverted pyramid theory. That means the most important (newsworthy) details go at the top of the story – the lead – and then generally end with the least important. In the middle are details that fulfill the 5W and H requirements. There are two reasons for this writing style: one, to get reader interest; two so that editors can edit for space.

By following this method, you can bet the person reading or hearing the message will understand what is going on. Once that's accomplished they will either keep reading (let's hope), or they will exit the story with a base understanding and move on.

PANTRY TEST – WRITING FOR THE MASSES

On the other end of the target audience spectrum are those messages not aimed at a specific group but for a variety of people – a mass audience. These are short, specific messages that need no interpretation; if you see or hear it, you can identify with it.

Knowing how to create these messages is easy if you can pass "The Pantry Test". Let me explain:

Convenience stores and gas stations are everywhere. In our neck of the woods, the most common convenience store is called The Pantry – a place where we purchase gasoline, soft drinks, snacks and other items on the go. It's usually not a site where people hang around or "shop"; they get what they need and are out of there in five minutes. If you take a moment to observe the different customers going in and out of these stores, you will see a wide range of types, from the dregs to the well-to-do.

Large companies, employing hundreds of people, will have workers of varying ages and education levels just like customers frequenting a convenience store. You need to keep this in mind when developing a message for the masses.

To help you do this, consider using what I term as "The Pantry Test" – a succinct, understandable message that any person going to the Pantry will comprehend and empathize with. Generally speaking, every message should have these characteristics, but business communicators often are expected to craft messages for specific groups – thereby not always communicating to the masses.

HIERARCHICAL MESSAGING

CEOs and presidents at larger corporations are not accustomed to creating messages that floor employees will comprehend. They know what they want to express and can do so very well for their peers, but they lack the expertise to communicate to the shop floor. Developing a message that everyone understands, regardless of the medium for which to do it, is one of the reasons why there are corporate communicators.

The optimal method of getting a CEO's message across is through face-to-face interaction. But if you are part of an organization employing thousands of people scattered across the globe, it's inconceivable to believe all of your employees will get such an opportunity. So, when most CEO messages arrive via a letter or PowerPoint presentation, communicators are likely to pass them along verbatim.

However, when local businesses receive a lengthy letter or presentation from the CEO – it might be worthwhile to edit it. Of course, some corporate communication departments do not take kindly to changing the messages they penned for their CEO, so one must take precautions in doing so. In all likelihood, someone at the top generated the presentation/message for the CEO's audience and was advised to pass it down the food chain – as is.

The types of corporate messages most likely to be edited are typically PowerPoint presentations and documents four pages or longer. It is common to receive PowerPoint presentations 25-30 slides in length, especially those relating to business objectives. Granted, there are plenty of graphs, but the graphs themselves are sometimes difficult for folks to figure out. The ideal setting would be to have a corporate communicator whose sole job is to recreate the presentation for a different target audience – those persons operating the machines. But it might be wishful thinking since that requires more personnel.

So, the best thing a communicator can do is to contact the corporate people and get their blessing to edit the documents. The obvious comeback from corporate is to say no and just send it to employees as is. But if they are responsive to the suggestion, give it some edit time, and then send the new version to them to get their endorsement.

LET'S BE TRANSPARENT

The big buzz word these days for what is considered to be fruitful communication in the business setting is "transparency." Being transparent essentially suggests we'll tell everybody what we want them to hear and then profess to being approachable and sincere about a given subject. It's acceptable conjecture, but oftentimes attempts at being transparent are unsuccessful because people do not know what to be transparent about. (In some cases the word "transparency" is used as an excuse to cover up what should not have been said in the first place.)

From a newspaper reporter's perspective, transparency is crucial if he or she wants readers to be aware of what is occurring in their community – it's what they do for a living. They strive to know secrets by gleaning as much information as possible from the subject or interviewee. If reporters are too conservative, they can get "scooped" by another news organization, so holding back on information can be detrimental to their respective newspapers and to themselves.

The rules are a bit different for company communicators. As the business communicator, you are constantly examining how much and what type of news you want employees to know, sans confidential information. There is a line between "public" and proprietary information and, frankly, some employees can't handle knowing too much. The business communicator's job is to decide what can be public (transparent) and what needs to stay behind closed doors.

No matter how "transparent" a company or business claims to be, the communicator and their fellow co-workers will only be privy to a portion of confidential information. And, honestly, there's nothing wrong with that. Sometimes being transparent is telling people you can't tell them anything. There's no harm in saying you know something but are not at liberty to divulge the information. In fact, communicators will earn considerably more respect if they say it in this manner.

The point here is that transparent communication is a method in which we keep employees informed about the inner workings of our business. It doesn't mean we have to tell them everything just that we plan to keep them informed about their operation.

Internal Communication Practices

The heart and soul of every business

Chapter 3

INTERNAL COMMUNICATION: IT'S THE BOMB!

There are generally two forms of communication processes that are recognized in the workplace: internal and external. External communication, sometimes referred to as public relations, is the means in which a business stays in contact with those outside the business – politicians, bankers, citizens, non-profits, etc. Internal communication is often described as a process in which information is disseminated to employees. The mechanisms for doing so might include closed-circuit televisions, dashboards, email, internal memos, meetings, newsletters and presentations – just to name a few.

(Internal communication, in fact, is much more than simply informing employees; it serves another important function, which is to provide business solutions. This form of communication will be reviewed in Chapter 5.)

If I had to choose which is more important, I would pick internal communication every day of the week and twice on Sunday. Without efficient internal communication, external communication efforts would be much more difficult to employ. Why? Because employees are the best external communication tools a business has. Further, the axiom, "an informed employee is a happy employee," is a reliable rule to live by.

This chapter includes several techniques communicators can use to "pump up" their internal information culture. However, before leaping into those practices, it's best to first audit and determine the types of internal communication processes the business already uses.

MAKING A COMMUNICATION EVOLUTION MODEL

English philosopher Edmund Burke once said, "Those who don't know history are destined to repeat it." The same goes for internal communication – a business needs to look at its historical approach to communication if it wants to make long-term, sustainable changes.

Not long ago, I developed what I termed the "Communication Evolution Model", a type of historical analysis of the internal communication culture and processes that a business has in place. Among the model's objectives was to review how messages were disseminated, when they were communicated, and the source preparing the communication.

I used this model at a local factory that opened in 1973, since management there wanted to increase the transparency of the business. Interviews were held with management team members, staff employees and floor workers to gather the history of their communication process. The model revealed that the entire organization operated like a stereotypical, untrusting union/management relationship for the better part of 30 years. Communication occurred mainly from management to the union executive board. In return, the board was expected to deliver the messages to their members. It was a lazy system that resulted in fragmented messages and misunderstandings. Sometimes, the messages that floor employees received were entirely inaccurate.

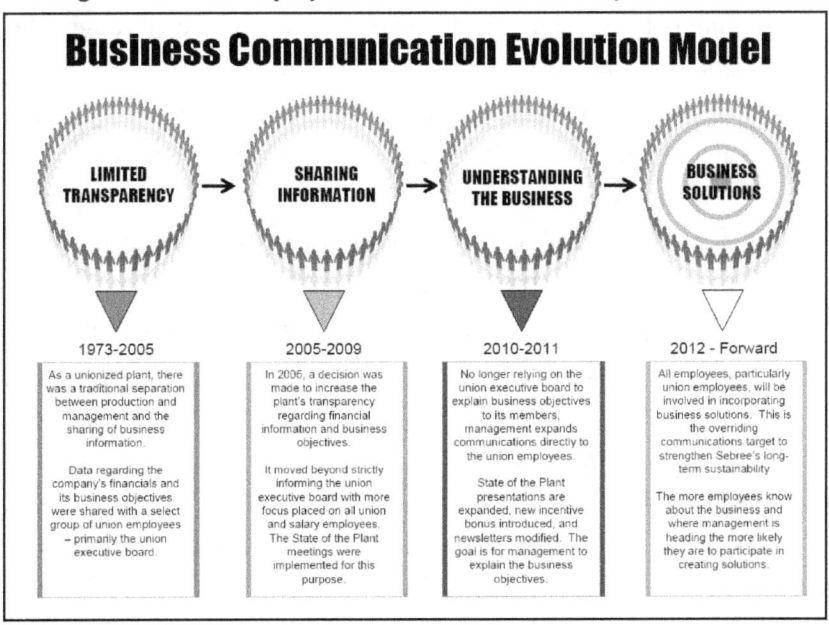

On top of that, there was not an "official" communicator, either. In fact, messages would come from several sources with each having their own writing styles; in other words, there was no consistency. Once the findings were studied, the following recommendations were made and followed:

- A communication team was developed.
- The old newsletter prepared by union staff members was overhauled and delivered on a monthly basis instead of quarterly. In fact, within six months it became a company produced document without assistance from the union.
- A television messaging system that was connected to monitors throughout the organization was upgraded and new messages began appearing daily instead of weekly or monthly.
- When union leaders and management met once a month to discuss business, the communicator recorded minutes and made them available to all employees. No longer did they work in a vacuum.
- Internal messages and memos were routed through the communicator.
- Department presentations were reviewed by the communicator the first year to encourage consistency in the way they were prepared.
- A new bulletin board system was installed at the front of the building where all employees passed.
- LED signs were installed at the company entrance and near the front gate.

As a result of these actions the communication improved dramatically within two years and considerably more when compared to 30 years earlier.

The model I developed is not all that significant – a company communicator can do the same thing by simply investigating the past and looking at the present. What's more important is to achieve management buy-in for incorporating the necessary changes needed to increase internal communication efficiency once the gaps are identified.

Now let's look at some practices communicators might add to the workplace.

STATE OF THE BUSINESS ADDRESS

Several years ago, a company I worked for was on the verge of changing general managers. Employees were informed that the present manager was taking another assignment, and a new guy would be taking his place within a couple of weeks. The departing manager was an even-tempered and gracious gentleman who built a reputation of obtaining consensus before big decisions were made. He was quite popular with the employees.

Taking his place was a guy who hailed from Europe. He was almost the exact opposite of the previous manager – a true Viking he was called – because he had impetuous reactions and didn't pause for a consensus. When he wanted something done, he was straight forward with his demand; employees were expected to do it and not question the motive. It was an amazing shift in narrative and quite a culture shock for everyone.

After a few months on the job, it was quite clear that he needed to upgrade his draconian interpersonal skills; he just didn't know how to relate to employees. It was truly his Achilles heel.

In an attempt to alleviate this growing problem, the HR department recommended to him that we inaugurate a series of "State of the Plant" presentations for all employees, where he could meet everyone face-to-face and provide a snapshot of our current production and financial results. Further, he could properly introduce himself, offer a personal story, and then shake hands with everyone.

The State of the Plant presentation we recommended might be compared to the U.S. president's State of the Nation address, where the president talks about the previous year and what he has planned for the future. The idea was to hold several 30 minute sessions over a two-week period so that our new manager could talk with all 650 employees.

The sessions were organized in this manner:
- The plant manager introduced himself and then asked every person attending to do the same – provide their name, where they worked, how long they had been at the business, and what they wanted the business to look like in five years.
- Next, the manager provided his annual business objectives with the assistance of a PowerPoint presentation of about 10 slides. The slides served as a placeholder for his thoughts and didn't contain all the information he wanted to convey.
- At the end, he opened up the floor for any questions the employees might have.

Presentations such as these are not awe inspiring nor are they unique to the business world. The most important aspect is they bring the manager down to the floor level, and that is what employees are looking for.

The key to these presentations is to make sure they are not very long. Remember, a person's attention span is in the area of seven minutes before they begin to tune out. It's best to incorporate no more than 10 slides containing highlights – not the actual presentation. This will force your presenter to speak from the heart and not read everything.

And here's another tip, don't provide copies of the presentation until after the meeting to avoid distractions from the speech itself. It can be disruptive to the speaker when people are flipping pages.

A SUCCINCT POWERPOINT PRESENTATION

One computer software program that communicators shouldn't be without is PowerPoint, the benchmark tool for developing and displaying business presentations. PowerPoint is a graphics program normally bundled with Microsoft Office programs Word and Excel. Word is used for writing articles, papers, reports…etc. and Excel is a spreadsheet program commonly utilized for financial purposes. Each, though, can be purchased separately.

PowerPoint allows users to develop a series of "slides" that are often presented through an LCD projector hooked to a computer. It allows the user to develop speaker notes, handouts and outlines of each slide. They can also edit documents, manipulate clipart, imbed animations, and add music.

From the design perspective, PowerPoint comes with several presentation templates available in its software package where users may choose a design and fill in the blanks, so to speak. For example, open PowerPoint, click "New" and the user will notice a menu that pops up where he or she can choose a blank presentation or a design template. If choosing the latter, a list of templates will appear, allowing the person to select a design.

(There are thousands of third party software templates available, if one was to forage the internet. Moreover, there are plenty of templates available at no cost, especially on Microsoft's online template website where the company and individuals post them.)

Here are some key points in developing a presentation:
- Above all, keep in mind PowerPoint presentations are there to support the presenter, not to be the main attraction. That's why the communicator should insist that presentations have no more than 10 slides. Simplicity is the rule of the thumb.
- Take advantage of bullet points in slides. Don't expand on a topic and expect the audience to read an overabundance of information. An appropriate number is about four or five

bullets per slide – and each one should be no more than a 10-word sentence.
- Use one font throughout the presentation – maybe Arial or Times. Keep in mind, if an eccentric font is used on one computer, the font file may not be embedded in the system on a different computer. If that's the case, the computer will replace it with a courier font, and that can totally ruin the design.
- Try incorporating photographs into the presentation. That's as easy as copying a photo and pasting it onto the slide.
- Use clip art sparingly. Preferably, purchase a clip art package or find some free clipart on the internet. The clipart preinstalled on PowerPoint is cheesy and looks amateurish.
- Animation can add wonders to a presentation, if used on rare occasions. PowerPoint allows the user to make text bounce and/or fly from corners or transition from one slide to another. One can make objects move around and follow a path. It is a great feature, but it can also be distracting, so be cautious when trying it.
- Stay away from background music or sound effects.
- Before delivering the presentation, try rehearsing it first. A common mistake presenters make is to discuss information from a slide that is yet to be seen. In other words, they get ahead of themselves. When they finally get to that slide, they feel as though they must cover the information again. As a result, their delivery time goes beyond what was planned.

COMMUNICATING DURING LAYOFFS

The hardest business decision a company is forced to make, short of closing, is to announce an employee cutback. No matter how it's presented – as a reduction in force, curtailment, layoff, or tightening of the belt – there's not a win-win circumstance in this case. The best a communicator can do is to ease the pain and keep everyone informed of what is transpiring.

Generally speaking, the mood inside the company is quite somber when a layoff is being planned. Not only are targeted employees feeling grief, it also negatively affects their co-workers who are fortunate enough to make the cut. Losing a job is one of the most traumatic events in a person's life – it ranks right up there with divorce – so the business needs to be sympathetic with everyone concerned.

The most important communication piece to develop in preparation for a layoff is an elevator speech – a two or three paragraph announcement about the layoff that is verbally delivered to all employees by the manager(s). This message's framework normally contains elements of the five W's and H and focuses solely on the subject at hand.

Here is an example elevator speech:

As you may be aware, the widget industry across the United States is suffering through an unprecedented downturn in production due to the dwindling health of the global economy. Unfortunately, our company has not been immune to these circumstances and has been dealing with the effects for the past several months.

As business analysts have determined that this downturn is likely to continue through the end of the year, (Company's Name) management team has made the decision to institute a minimal employee layoff on April 1. This is a very difficult choice we have to make, but our efficiency measures implemented earlier in the year have not satisfied our budgetary requirements.

In that regard, the company's human resources department will begin notifying 45 employees within the next two days that they will be laid off for an undetermined amount of time. It is our goal to return these employees to the workforce as soon as possible.

Those who assume it's somewhat callous not to warn people as far in advance as possible must understand the complexities of getting ready for the layoff. There are numerous HR issues to be aware of, including: potential state or federal notices, deciding how much more work others will have to assume, unemployment issues, potential retirements…etc. Plus, a business will want to avoid seeing valuable people depart the business – those they planned to keep on board.

Knowing that questions about the layoff will surface, determine in advance whether to share any more information than the elevator speech. Also, develop a list of questions and answers based on what employees will want to know. This will allow management to have something to refer to in case they get hit with questions. As an employee I would want to know more than the elevator speech:

- How did you determine who would get laid off?
- Will there be any incentive packages offered?
- Can I take a voluntary layoff?
- Will I have health insurance during the layoff?
- Will a layoff affect my seniority status?
- What other options has the company considered besides a layoff?
- Will I qualify for unemployment insurance?
- Can I use my accrued vacation and then take layoff status?
- Is there a chance that I will have the same job when I return to work?

These are just a few questions that might be posed by employees, so it's best to have responses before the announcement is made. Obviously, management won't have all the answers, but it is best to be as prepared as possible.

COMMUNICATING A COMPANY ACQUISITION

When one company takes over another, there's apprehension and anxiety in the air among employees who are part of the company being purchased. For one, the company taking over usually forces its superiority on the smaller company because it's now the bigger brother. That means some employees of both companies will harbor the perception that the new owners are wiser and more efficient; otherwise, why would they be buying the business, right?

The communicator for the company being taken over will play a key role in the transition process by relaying and disseminating information from the buying company to his own employees. Actually, the communicator will feel as though he is straddling a fence – doing what the new company tells him to do but being loyal to the old company and its employees until the deal is finalized.

News of the sale may cause employees to entertain their greatest professional fears by first thinking layoffs and job eliminations. It happens in many cases because companies do not purchase another company to keep the status quo – they buy other businesses because they see synergies and other cost savings measures, which is what attracted them in the first place. On the other side of the aisle, the acquiring company's employees will have concerns, too, such as whether their workload will increase, or if they have to transfer to another location.

Employees will be hungry for any news about their new owners and will probably take it upon themselves to perform research online about the company and its leaders. They may contact colleagues, the media, and the new company itself to find any slither of information. This is also the time when rumors begin to spread about the new company.

Before employees take it upon themselves to "communicate" to their own co-workers what they have found, it's best to be preemptive and consider some of these ideas:

- First and foremost, make sure all messages about the new company are explicitly positive. The purchasing company may not be up to the standards everyone is used to but, in no uncertain terms, should it be self-evident that there are reservations about their management style. A communicator's job is to accentuate the positive and leave no doubt who is in command.
- Create a fact sheet about the new company that underscores what employees will initially want to know: the official name, size, financials, locations of other sister plants, employees, products, et al. If it is a publicly traded company, filling in the blanks will be much easier.
- If the new company is far superior in size and credentials, consider creating a company comparison chart demonstrating the advantages of being owned by a larger company. Maybe the pension is better; the health insurance is enhanced; or there could be opportunities for employees to transfer to other locations – on their own terms.
- Publish a special edition newsletter devoted entirely to the transaction. It can include some of the information mentioned in the previous bullets, but it will be more powerful if the CEO can be interviewed and photographed.

Periodically review how well the communication is being received by employees. The best way to do that is to talk with colleagues and find out if they have any suggestions that will help keep them informed.

MAKE EMAIL WORK FOR YOU

There's a love/hate relationship with email. When the concept was first indoctrinated into the business setting, getting an email was like receiving a UPS or Federal Express package – it was rather exciting.

Boy, times have changed.

Email has become a hindrance to many people because they receive too much of it. Due to the proliferation of computer viruses and hoax messages, it is becoming difficult to ascertain which emails to open for fear of exposing the bowels of Pandora's Box.

Business communicators know that emails play a pivotal role for spreading a message, and it is an avenue for inducing employee involvement. There's also a flipside as well; relying solely on email for communicating can cause a dividing line and actually pull people away from each other. This is another reason why business email should be written wisely and for a purpose.

A rule to remember with reference to emails is, they do not convey more than typed words – they bare no emotion. (Okay, I understand a smiley emoticon at the end of a sentence is supposed to lead a person into an emotional state of happiness – but we're talking business here and not personal emails.) When writing email, first and foremost, keep them short and to the point – maybe a couple of paragraphs.

So, how do you write an email that won't be deleted either by accident or on purpose?

One idea is to color code the subject line in a way that highlights the message's importance. For example, use a green border for messages sharing conventional information like an upcoming meeting; yellow for those offering caution and needs one's attention; and red for those requiring immediate action. It is a very reliable system to consider.

Tips for avoiding email pitfalls

While communicators should not be assigned to be the company's email policeman, more than likely they will be involved – at least through internal memos written specifically about email usage. Even more, Human Resources may rely on the communicator to offer information about email etiquette. In that case, here are some tips to consider sharing with employees:

- Avoid writing email messages when anger is involved. Flying off the handle, while it temporarily relieves some of the anger, can turn out to be a terrible mistake because once it's on paper it becomes discoverable.
- If something confidential needs to be written, ensure the email is "encrypted" so that it cannot be forwarded; most email programs have this tool available.
- Keep any attachments to less than 1 megabyte in size. This might require a file compression program, something that can be downloaded at no cost.
- Auto responders are a nice way to ensure that the intended recipient receives the email; however, don't overdo it. If the email may be used in some type of legal action down the road, then it might be appropriate to ask for a "read receipt." Doing this for non-essential emails is a pain for the recipient. Moreover, recipients may become suspicious of the sender's intentions if they are continuously asked for read receipts.
- Discourage emails that express the writer's feelings about a touchy subject – say religion or politics. Nobody cares!
- Discourage soon-to-be retirees or employees leaving for another job from writing a sobbing message of thanks. The best way to stop this before it happens is through an email policy. (I've read no telling how many emails from employees casually bashing management styles before they leave for another job.)

BUILDING & MAINTAINING AN INTRANET SITE

Most organizations of 10 or more employees are often connected to a computer network interface that allows them to swap email, share software, hard drive space, and exchange documents.

Networking has a distinct advantage for companies and employees because it increases work productivity.

Another vital aspect of networking is the ability to build an internal website; most often referred to as an Intranet. It is similar to the World Wide Web except it is only accessible by employees or persons directly connected with the business. An in*ter*net site, on the other hand, is accessible for the general public – for example a .com, .edu, or .gov address.

Intranet sites at larger corporations contain many tentacles that consist of a primary site, while their satellite businesses create and operate their own intranet as part of the corporate site. With proper security measures, intranets are often available to employees who can remotely sign in at work, from their homes, or through some type of mobile accessible device.

(Since this book is about workplace communication, the development of an intranet will only be referred to in this section. There are numerous books and university degrees available on building an intranet, including all the intricate details of TCP/IP protocols, web servers, security issues and other infrastructure demands.)

The main challenge in building an intranet site is to ensure that the necessary network infrastructure is available – including content management software, firewalls, a server, bandwidth…etc. These technical aspects are normally handled by the IT department. For this practice, and for the sake of argument, we'll assume those matters will not serve as roadblocks.

The first and most instinctive decision that will be made about the intranet site is to post links to internal documents such as expense report forms and vacation requests, calendars, department news, and stock quotes. That's a great start, but here are some additional ideas:

- Chat Rooms: Establish a dedicated "room" where employees can log in and communicate live with other employees – oftentimes with colleagues from around the world.
- Blogs: A blog is similar to a personal diary and usually focuses on a particular topic – say like a manager's notes about the business. The author usually updates the blog on a regular basis – sometimes by the hour or every day or so. It's mostly published in reverse-chronological order.
- Employee Announcements: this may include awards given to workers, new positions being created, work anniversaries, employee weddings, birth announcements and birthdays.
- Business Announcements: one or two paragraph articles about an event occurring inside the business.
- Employee Feedback: another well-received idea is to implement a feedback mechanism where employees can leave anonymous questions. In turn, management answers the question, and then it is posted for all to see. (This idea is discussed in the Employee Feedback chapter.)

Whatever the choices are for content, the most important job once a site is established is to systematically update it so it doesn't become stagnant. If a communicator happens to let an intranet site go dormant, it becomes little more than a gateway to the internet, and then it will take time before it can once again earn employees' loyalty and interest.

TEACH BUSINESS BASICS TO YOUR EMPLOYEES

Not everyone at work is business savvy or holds a deep understanding about how a company handles its finances. For many, they just assume companies run their operations in a comparable manner as an individual – one earns money, puts it in the bank, and then withdraws it to pay the bills.

Finances are tricky where businesses are concerned, even more so for public companies scrutinized by analysts and auditors. Finance department workers spend countless hours taking care of taxes, depreciation, inventory, payrolls, department budgets and a myriad of other needs that will keep the business on the up and up. On the other hand, the extent of financial involvement for most other employees begins and ends with their paychecks. The reason for that is because no one has taken the time to explain how the company's finances work.

A conscientious communicator should set a goal to inform employees how the company makes money and where it spends it. By following some simple communication steps, the business can help eliminate common misconceptions that plague management during an economic downturn or some other crucial event.

For example, some uninformed employees believe earned profits are stashed in a local bank to be withdrawn when needed. "You have plenty of money, why don't you fix the problem," is the standard battle cry for weary production employees who wrongly believe their local business keeps all the profit it earns.

Local managers do not have an ATM card with clearance to withdraw a half million dollars for a project – they work their way through a requisition process to prove they need a piece of equipment. Because that takes days, weeks, or even months, employees can get discouraged by having to continue to work with old, unsafe equipment. They might wonder why the production manager doesn't call a local equipment company to have a new forklift sent over.

To better inform and teach employees about simple business finance, the communicator should develop a series of articles in the business newsletter or in a PowerPoint presentation that focuses on "How the company makes money" and "How the company spends money." These are two simplified questions that, when answered, will enlighten employees. Let's look at both of these questions separately and in very simple terms vis-à-vis the Pantry Test.

How does a company make money?

That's easy: they sell a product or service at a higher price tag than what it costs to produce it. Simple, huh? But wait a minute; do employees understand how to acquire customers? Do they know who their company's customers are? How do production managers know how many widgets to make? These are questions, among many others, that can help employees better understand the company's financial condition.

How does a company spend money?

There's a lot more that goes into spending money than employees fully understand. For example, do they know about fluctuating material costs for making a product? Are they aware that the business has utility and fuel bills, machinery breakdown costs, employee wages, unemployment insurance, consultants, inventory, training costs, attorneys' fees and currency differences?

Managers might be amazed to find out how little employees know about their workplace – even those who've been with the business for a couple of decades. Employees will rarely volunteer to demonstrate their lack of knowledge about finances – they would just as soon allow the bosses to think they are in tune with how everything works. It's the epitome of, and another way of looking at, the "don't ask, don't tell" philosophy.

So, what can the communicator do to inform them – to alleviate their anxiety that they could be put on the spot at sometime or another? One, the communicator can write a series of articles in the company's newsletter about finances. Fox example:

- Article 1: An overview of the business model, including managers' business objectives – the reason they do what they do.

- Article 2: Focus on how the company earns money and how profits are utilized by answering some of the questions posed above. If the business is part of a larger organization, then explain how income is diverted to the parent company.
- Article 3: Provide employees with an overview of the top customers – how they utilize the company's products or services.
- Article 4: Describe company expenditures – where, when and why the company spends its money. Along with the article, create a graphic illustration to help readers comprehend this part of finances. Try this: use a dollar bill background and draw horizontal lines up the dollar bill depicting how a percentage of the money is allocated for items such as salaries, materials, capital improvements, profit…etc. Next to the graph, show that 30 cents is for salaries, 10 cents for materials, 10 cents for capital improvements and so on. Using an illustration in this manner will be more acceptable than verbiage about millions of dollars. Everyone can relate to how a dollar is spent.

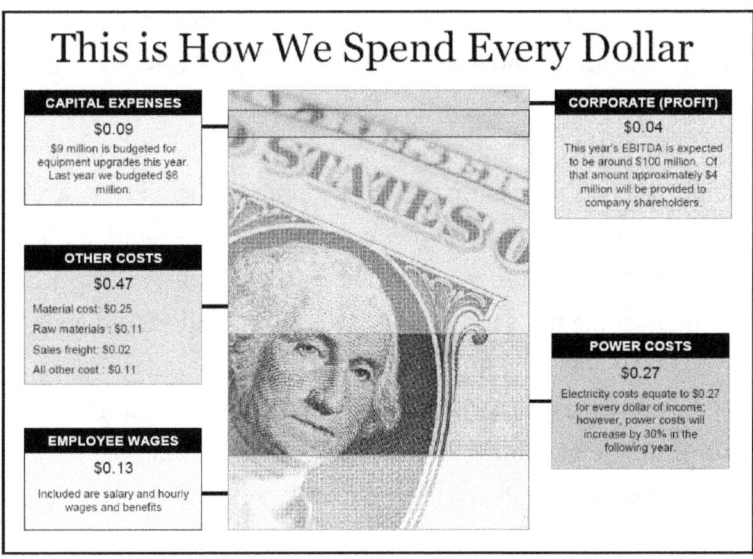

Here's another idea that works:

Some people are better visual learners or prefer to hear about a topic than reading about it. In addition to the articles, work with the finance department to create a 30-minute presentation about company finances. Be ready to see a room full of people.

TELEPHONES: SETTING UP AN INFO LINE

A relatively simple and inexpensive internal communication tool any business can incorporate is a telephone messaging system for employees. All a person has to do is dial a specific phone number to access a one to two minute recorded message about their place of employment. It only takes a dedicated telephone number and about 15 minutes of time each day to keep it updated. The names of such systems vary by location so let's be somewhat generic and call our example the "Employee Info Line."

The first item of business for establishing an info line is to dedicate a telephone account either through the company's telephone networking system or with a telephone company. (Larger businesses will have a bank of phone numbers available to them that are divvied out to new employees.) Assign a phone number to the info line that is easy to remember and accessible internally and externally – just like a standard phone number.

Once the phone line is established, the telecommunication administrator should provide the communicator with an access code so only he or she can post a message. Listeners should not be allowed to reply or access other phone numbers through the Info Line. They should hear the message, and then the phone call should end.

When the infrastructure is ready, the final task is to record a message. As recommended earlier in this book, keep messages short and to the point – maybe a minute or two. The speaker's demeanor should be upbeat as well – showing a smile as she records the message.

The determining factor on whether the Info Line is successful will be the content – recording what sparks employee interest. This may include a safety message, company stock quote, special events (such as blood drive or United Way campaign), emergency messages, production numbers, job opportunities, and/or new policy announcements.

When recording the message don't try to be a perfectionist by re-recording several times until the message is flawless. For some people, a simple mumble will cause them to start the whole thing over. Really, nobody cares that a word or two is jumbled – it just sounds natural.

Try promoting the system by writing a newsletter story about its inception. Another idea is to make small stickers resembling a telephone with the Info Line's phone number printed on it.

LUNCH AND LEARN

Bar none, the best kind of communication is face-to-face interaction. Nothing is more effective than to sit with another person and have a conversation about work. As uncomplicated as that might appear to be, it's sometimes easier said than done, especially with larger businesses. The chances are slim that a general manager can regularly chat with individual employees – that's why email is so popular.

Most face-to-face conversations between a high ranking company person and front-line employees usually occur during impromptu visits to the front office or when the manager makes a visit to the floor. In some cases, at least at the corporate level, it's quite rare for a CEO to visit one of his or her manufacturing facilities.

To promote transparency in the business setting, employees need to see and hear from the people running their business. This type of interaction gives them a greater sense of belonging. One way to do this is establish a program called "Lunch and Learn," which is basically an opportunity for a manager to eat lunch with a selected group of employees and to participate in a 30-minute roundtable discussion. The end in mind is to share ideas and to get to know employees better – not to make major announcements.

Before organizing such a meeting, first determine what type of outcome is desired. Is it a chance for employees to get something off their collective chests? Are there production or financial issues that need to be discussed? Or is it simply a chance to allow employees and the manager to become better acquainted? Whatever the reason, the communicator will play a significant role in prepping the manager.

Next, decide how often to hold a Lunch and Learn; it can be weekly, monthly or bimonthly depending on the number of employees. Ideally, it's best to have every employee participate at least once during the year. So, if there are 500 people, it would be wise to have weekly or bi-weekly lunches. My recommendation is to keep the number of invited guests to no more than 25 – a smaller amount is better and more appealing for this practice.

Depending upon how chatty the manager is will directly correlate with how much preparation is needed. An introverted manager will require more preparation time, as she might not feel at ease with frank discussions. But, if the manager knows how to handle an audience, organizing the activity can be a breeze.

Next, collaborate with the manager to determine the topic(s) to be discussed. Since the purpose of the luncheons is to have face-to-face interaction, stay away from pre-printed material and overhead presentations – let her do the talking. And, above all, be prepared for unexpected questions or negative reactions. One can't predict when, or if, controversy might strike.

By all means, don't shy away from asking negative people to these luncheons, otherwise it will appear as if you are trying to skirt the "real" issues. The manager must listen intently and then respond to the comments and questions.

Start the program at 11:30 or 12:00, with lunch provided for all attendees. As workers arrive, ensure the manager greets them and asks them to find a seat. If possible, try to keep groups of employees who normally work together away from the same tables. Otherwise, this can only encourage unruliness if frustration is expected to be vented.

Before the day is wrapped, take a few photographs that can be used in the business newsletter and then write a cutline stating what the meeting was about. This will serve as way to inform employees how the lunches are configured.

MEETINGS – THE NECESSARY EVIL

Have you experienced the resounding gratification of participating in an office or organizational meeting where the topics were noticeably outlined, addressed, and understood by those attending? You know, one of those invigorating meetings where the people attending were interactive, productive and respectful of each other's opinion? On the other end of the spectrum, what about sitting through an afternoon meeting listening to judgmental and unsupportive employees who would rather be surfing the internet?

Business meetings are a way of life, and they will continue to happen until the world comes to an end. There's really nothing wrong with that, either – unless meetings are being held just for the sake of having them which, in many cases, is what happens in the workplace. Problems associated with unproductive meetings surface when there is inadequate planning or preparations prior to each gathering. These are issues that a communicator can correct.

Pick the right time for a meeting

If the plan is to have weekly or monthly meetings, try holding them on a Monday or Tuesday, since this gives employees an opportunity to complete assignments by the end of the week and to have discussions with other employees.

A preferable time to start meetings is 9 a.m., 10 a.m. or 3 p.m. Since most employees arrive between 7-8 a.m., you want to give them time to settle in and answer email. By 9 or 10 a.m., people are jacked up on coffee, tea or soft drinks and their focus is sharper – a great time to dig into their creative side. By 3 p.m., employees are looking to finish the day with a success so they will be attentive and willing to accept assignments.

(You might wonder why I don't recommend starting meetings at 11, 1 or 2 o'clock. Well, about halfway into the 11 a.m. meeting employees tend to get hungry, and their minds begin to focus on food. At 1 or 2 p.m. people are satiated and tend to lose focus.)

Try hard to keep meetings to one hour or less, if possible; people hate long meetings. Besides, the chances of redundant comments increase exponentially after that point anyway.

Establishing an agenda to get work done

One of the most overlooked and undervalued components of workplace meetings are agendas – the list of topics the leader plans to address. Agendas are usually prepared by the person running the meeting, or by a committee, and then sent to the participants in advance. At least that's the preferable way to do it. However, don't be surprised if the agenda is created at the meeting.

An effective agenda will list the topics to be discussed in a step-by-step manner but not necessarily in the order of importance. Keep in mind that the arrangement can be altered at the beginning of the meeting to support someone who needs to leave early.

Once the completed agenda is sent to participants, it is prudent to also include any information pertinent to the subjects that will be discussed. For example, if the meeting is about the department's budget, then send the budget along with the agenda to participants in advance so that they can study it.

The central aspect of putting an agenda together is to make sure it's followed.

Being on time

Start meetings on time! If the leader gets into the habit of starting at 3:05 or 3:10 because he or she is waiting on someone to arrive, then the precedent has been set and the next time somebody else will be late.

Speaking of being on time, if the leader has a decent relationship with the participants, here's something fun – with serious overtones – to stress the point of timeliness. Keep a pack of neon Post-It notes nearby – maybe bright pink or orange – and if a person is late to start the meeting or takes too long of a break, write "written warning" on a note and put it in a spot where they are sitting. Even if they are standing just a few feet away but are not in their seat at the time the meeting reconvenes, put the "warning" in their spot anyway.

I co-facilitated a half-day workshop with a consultant who taught me this trick. Our department was notorious for people taking too much time at break, lunch or just coming in late. When we did this during our workshop, those who got one of the pink notes with a written warning on it were actually shocked.

There's one of two immediate reactions that will happen: the person getting the note will take it in stride, or they will get perturbed. Either way, the participant receiving the "discipline" will get the message from that point forward. The majority of time, though, it seems to draw a laugh or snicker from other participants.

Invite those who will make a difference

Who should be invited to the meeting? The correct answer should be only those with direct involvement in the subject matter – not supplementary participants. If it's a brainstorming session, keep it to five or less – and be choosy about the five people. Whoever is selected, it is crucial they are active participants. The guy down the hall searching for meetings to attend so he can justify his time, pass on him.

Once the meeting starts, ask participants to help develop guidelines on how to facilitate the meeting. If attendees have a say in how the meeting flows, including listing proper etiquette, it will be much easier to administer. Some respectable etiquette techniques include:

- Silencing cellular telephones.
- Don't check email.
- Allow the person speaking to finish his or her thought.
- Raise a hand instead of shouting a comment.
- Don't tap or click a pen. Sometimes people have no idea they are doing these things, and they won't recognize it unless it's verbalized.
- Ask participants to attend the entire meeting. Rarely should they be given a "get out of jail free" card.

Most importantly, participants should anticipate that they will receive some type of assignment or responsibility regarding the topics discussed. The leader should then follow up afterwards to see how they are progressing.

Set the tone early

Once everybody is at the table and the etiquette rules have been established, you might introduce a brief safety topic. It could include a weather report if storms are on the horizon or maybe something concerning employee health or the environment. By referring to safety at the onset of a meeting, especially in a manufacturing environment, employees will come to appreciate that someone cares for their well being.

Next, assign a person to take notes during the meeting, which would probably be the leader, unless someone volunteers. Use a computer and overhead to display the notes as they are written. This technique helps in a few ways: first, by typing notes on an overhead, everybody is on the same page – figuratively speaking. Second, there's a reduced chance that a participant will misunderstand the topic or assignment. Third, the notes can also serve as the meeting minutes so the leader doesn't need to spend time after the meeting deciphering hand written notes. (Another tip: type a participant's name in red under the topic if they are responsible for a related assignment).

At the end of the agenda, perform a "wrap-up" or summary to make sure everybody's together. It only takes a few minutes. If it's a longer meeting ask participants what worked well and what did not.

ADDRESSING WORKPLACE RUMORS

As common, curious people, most of us like to hear a juicy rumor about something happening in the workplace – whether the subject is strictly business or about an individual. Workplace rumors often start when someone overhears part of a conversation between two other people and then tries to fill in the blanks. Another way they begin is when someone maliciously spreads false information.

In whatever fashion they originate, rumors are essentially filled with unverified information that is often taken out of context. Common topics might include somebody's job being on the hot seat; a big customer is cancelling orders; the business is selling; a disgruntled manager is leaving; or Jane and John are having an affair. Whether they prove to be true or not, rumors can develop a life of their own and can spread out of control if they are not quickly dispelled.

So what's the big deal with hearing or spreading a rumor? Gossip, rumors – whatever you want to call them – can generate immediate, harmful ramifications and cause employees to lose their concentration, enthusiasm and motivation. It's especially troubling to the person being targeted. People participate in the rumor mill as a way to connect with co-workers; it gives them fulfillment in being a part of the conversation. Besides, there's no pressure to be accurate.

So, can something be done to stop rumors from starting? Probably not in the short term, even if the general manager sends out a memo telling employees they can no longer gossip. Thus, a continuous challenge for communicators is to keep the rumor mill in check so that they do not negatively affect daily business or, worse yet, end up in the media.

But there is a long-term solution to quelling rumors and that is for the business to be proactive and attack the problem by fostering an environment where employees are encouraged to ask questions about work-related gossip. Managers should listen to employees' concerns and then talk to them as much as possible. If the rumor harbors some truth but the subject can't be discussed, it's best to confirm you heard the information but are not at liberty to discuss it at any great length. Employees will appreciate the honesty. (See Chapter 10 on employee feedback mechanisms.)

When the workplace acknowledges employees' concerns, and managers listen attentively to them, workers will soon learn they don't need to be obsessed about topics they have little or no control over. They will remain curious but won't take it personally.

PUBLISHING AN EMPLOYEE PHOTO CALENDAR

Everybody uses a calendar – they are part of our everyday lives. Maybe we use them for planning events, posting reminders of errands we need to run, or sometimes just to remember what day it is. Calendars come in all shapes and sizes and feature themes like golf courses, animals, cities, vehicles, swimsuit models – you name it. The point is, they're everywhere – and they are relevant. So why not take advantage of this significant communication tool and create a calendar for employees? It's really easy – and you're sure to get a least a year's worth of pleasure from them.

Let me provide a couple scenarios for producing a calendar:

I once worked for a company that valued employee safety so much that each worker's daily activities had to include some type of safety recognition. Management even went so far as to give away smoke detectors, weather radios, fire extinguishers, and first aid kits to all of its employees. Then someone came up with a great idea of making a calendar geared towards safety awareness – a Christmas gift we would give to employees and family members.

After a brief discussion we decided our best move was to get kids involved. So, we prepared a flyer requesting employees' children or grandchildren in grades K-3 if would they like to draw a picture for us to use in the calendar. It had to be about safety and we offered examples such as a fire emergency, severe weather, driving safely, or wearing a helmet while riding a bike. In return, we would provide a $50 savings bond to those children whose pictures we used in the calendar.

We were inundated with drawings. If truth be told, we actually received more than we had hoped for – so many that we couldn't use them all. We picked the best ones for each month and worked with a printer to publish them. By December 1, we had the new calendars in hand.

After the third year of printing the safety calendars, we switched gears and created calendars featuring photographs taken by our employees. Once again, we solicited photos, but they had to be taken by the employee or a family member. The other requirement was that the photos had to be snapped outdoors, and no one could be in them. (We didn't want to go through the red tape of getting prior approval from people in the photo.)

We received approximately 40 pictures – enough that we were able to match the photo with the appropriate month. As an example, snowy pictures were used for December and January, flowers were used in April and May, and a close-up of a spider in a web was used for October. We actually had two calendars made: one for employees that included shift schedules and one for the general public (no schedules).

The business has continued to make special calendars since then.

Desktop Publishing

Creating a self-sustaining communication system

Chapter 4

ESTABLISHING YOUR DESKTOP SYSTEM

Communicators searching for a cost-effective printing method to keep employees informed should seriously consider adopting a desktop publishing system. With suitable equipment and software, they can write, design and print tangible products at work such as brochures, newsletters, cards, flyers and posters instead of outsourcing the work to expensive printers.

And that's not all; it will give communicators total influence over their own content – how it looks, last-second changes to articles, or the opportunity to publish a story that would otherwise have to wait another month.

To enter the world of publishing the communication department will need the following:

1) A desktop computer with lots of memory, a massive hard drive, top-quality graphics card, and a 23-inch monitor. (Cost: $1,500).
2) A superior printer, capable of printing 11x17 papers, preferably on both sides simultaneously. (Cost: $5,000-$7,500)
3) A desktop publishing software kit and word processing program (Cost: $500)

Also, consider purchasing a second video monitor for around $200. Two monitors sitting side by side grants a person the ability to work simultaneously on different programs without splitting screens or minimizing and maximizing programs on one monitor. Newer computers usually bundle a video card that supports two monitors – one as the primary monitor and then an auxiliary. If the computer isn't equipped with a graphics card to support two monitors, it only costs about $150 to install a second card.

With this equipment, the communicator is now ready to be an in-house publisher, capable of spitting out dozens of products ranging from newsletters and posters to quality memos. The $10,000 invested in this equipment will be returned many times over before anything needs replacing.

Another piece of equipment the communicator will need is a camera.

Photography today sure isn't what it used to be back before it entered the digital revolution in the mid-1990s. Instead of burning images on film, cameras began storing them on a small hard drive. Speculation now is that by 2020 camera film will no longer be produced.

The beauty of digital photography is the ability to take a picture, upload it to the computer, and then print it out within minutes. Most computers will have photo editing software that will allow the photographer to enhance the photo's appearance. If not, there are plenty of free ones available on the internet. Of course, some cameras allow editing on the camera itself.

The toughest job today is finding the appropriate camera to use. Digital photography has changed so quickly, causing the space between mediocre and high end equipment to become closer and closer. In film photography, there is a distinct variance between quality equipment and budget equipment. This isn't so much the case with digital cameras when you get down to brass tax.

The media, specifically online tech sites, want consumers to believe they must purchase the highest megapixel camera or they will miss out on beautiful photos. That is a bunch of malarkey, unless one plans to enlarge a picture to the size of Farrah Fawcett's famous swimsuit poster. When printing 5x7 pictures or using them in a newsletter, a person will find little distinction between 10 megapixel and 20 megapixel photos.

The market is inundated these days with $100-$200 digital cameras manufactured by dozens of companies. While professional photographers often stick with manufacturers who built their reputations on photography such as Canon and Nikon, the casual photographer might choose a camera on the lower end of the scale. Personally, I recommend purchasing an 8-10 megapixel camera with at least five times optical zoom, which can be found for well under $200. Even better, there are a host of cameras on reputable internet sites for less than $100.

The bottom line is this: it's not the cost of the camera that makes the photographer stand out…it is the photo!

CREATING NEWSLETTERS

Company newsletters are typically published for the general employee population and contain wide-ranging topics from finances and health care to feature stories and professional accomplishments. Their length may be a one-page document or a booklet with 36 pages or more. Most of them are published either monthly or quarterly.

Communication departments within the private sector will seldom employ a journalism professional to publish newsletters; thus, they are often written and produced by a human resources person whose primary responsibility might be coordinating benefits. If money is readily available, newsletter production may be assigned to an outside contractor who will put together a publication based on the company's needs. Some agencies will actually write the articles, design the newsletter, publish it, and distribute copies. I know one business that spends upwards to $100,000 annually to hire an agency to print and distribute a monthly, 12-page tabloid size newsletter to its 1,200 employees. The amount does not take into account the salary the editor receives for writing stories and taking photographs. It is an appealing publication, but rather expensive to produce. Consequently, it's not worth the money being put into it.

On the other hand, if a business is looking to save money and have more control of the information being printed, then it should strongly consider an internally produced newsletter. From the tangible perspective, it costs considerably less to print from within, a great feature for cost-conscious managers. But the real savings from publishing internally isn't tangible; it is the realization that the publication contains articles that may be only a day or two old – just like a local newspaper. In today's "now" culture, one or two-week old news doesn't hack it anymore. That's usually what a business gets from an externally produced newsletter.

At this point, let's look at some of the essentials for printing a nice newsletter:

Keep it Short and Sweet: The News Brevity Age

Today's journalism is much different than it was 30 years ago. Back then there was no internet, smart phones, blogs or a glut of news channels. Much of what was learned about news events came mostly from lengthy articles in newspapers and magazines. If someone wanted a lot of detail, it came from the printed word.

But then in the early 1980s, along came the USA Today newspaper and its industry changing design that focused on shorter news stories and lots of graphics. It was bright and colorful, which led to a large readership – eventually becoming the most widely circulated newspaper in the United States.

It happened because readers liked the look and variety. They could get succinct articles, graphics and photos that were just enough to fulfill their need-to-know. It didn't take long for other newspapers to notice USA Today's success as they began taking on similar characteristics – including design techniques and shorter articles.

Then in the 1990s, a little thing called the internet arrived and journalism began its reluctant transition to an on-line presence. By the middle of the next decade, there was a vast amount of news available on the internet, just as there were more than 100 cable television stations from which to choose. People didn't stay on one web site or TV news channels for very long as they found what they needed and moved on to another site. News organizations figured this out and adjusted their story length to shorter articles, news briefs and more graphics in hopes of keeping their audience coming back. Vis-à-vis, look at scrolling news at the bottom of news channels nowadays.

In the late 2000s, two other technological innovations advanced, promoted and reinforced shorter news articles: smart phones and computer tablets. With these toys we can now read articles while standing in line at the bank. If anything, we now have a fast food mentality for news.

To further prove we have entered the news brevity stage, look at the linguistic changes that are popular in today's culture. People won't even take time to write out sentences anymore. Think about it: when composing text messages people write LOL for Laugh Out Loud; OMG for Oh, My Gosh; and BFF for Best Friends Forever. And that is only a miniscule part of the digital dialogue. While teens appear to be the most affected by digital "journalism", people who grew up in the age of Walter Cronkite are being forced to change their ways of communicating – and it seems to be working out just fine.

In summary, business communicators should bear in mind that brief and simplistic news stories are more enticing to employees Thus, it's a good idea to write articles with no more than 250 words.

Inserting Photographs to Enhance Newsletters

Photographs are the most popular and powerful form of graphics used in company newsletters; in fact, they can easily outshine a news story. Why? Employees can relate to photos, especially when a co-worker is the featured subject. Similarly, employees like seeing themselves in print because it gives them a sense of importance. But most of all, photos are very simple to comprehend.

The best photographs are feature or spot photos that don't require employees to line up and smile. The traditional "grip and grin" pictures are necessary in some cases but they are so boring. Instead, communicators should get out of their comfort zone and take an intriguing photo of someone in action. .

To increase the chance of capturing a poignant photograph, here is a great tip: every so often take a walk throughout the workplace and snap some photographs of employees doing their jobs. People working on machinery make for great opportunities to get action photos. Another idea is to attend company functions or community service work where photo ops are plentiful.

However, if there's not much time to get an action shot or stage a photo, there is another option. Try purchasing photographs from an internet source such as Big Stock Photo. That may sound like blasphemy to die-hard photographers, but there are some great photos at this and other sites. For example, if a safety story is being written about pedestrian traffic, there are plenty of related photos that can be purchased for a dollar or two; just pay the fee, download it, and then position it with the article.

The Mighty Word! Using Fonts

Fonts, which consist of varying styles of a printed character, can make or break a message. A carefully written report, advertisement or newsletter can be ruined simply because the font used to display the message(s) was difficult to read. Therefore, it is vital to use a font that's easy on the eyes – and to stick with it.

Some publications never change their text or headline fonts. Others may tweak them a bit, but usually only once every few years. The point here is, be conservative in font usage and not go on some rampage by selecting different fonts based on mood (i.e., I feel happy today so I'm going to use a sissy font).

The primary font used in newspapers is Times New Roman or some variant of Times because it is easier to read. About the only time newspapers have a chance to use distinctive fonts is if they publish a feature story on the front page of an inside section. (In workplace communication, it's a bit more laissez-faire in using fonts, but it's still best to remain consistent.)

For printed material, choose a serif font such as Times or Garamond. Studies upon studies have been conducted by news outlets, and they know a serif font is best for writing and reading text. Sans serif fonts such as Arial, Helvetica and Verdana are useful for headlines and on-line web sites.

Computer users don't need to purchase fonts these days because they can be found without charge on the internet. Just type in "fonts" in a search engine and hundreds of links will pop up leading to complimentary fonts.

Use color stylishly

Here's my tip for utilizing color in a newsletter: think of a woman who sprays on perfume in the morning. If she uses just enough to tickle your fancy, you may want to get closer to acquire a heightened sense of smell. Now recall women who squirt perfume on so heavily a person can continue to smell them as they leave the building. Which one is more impressive? Use color with the same intentions as the woman who wears just enough perfume to arouse the olfactory senses.

Of course, the ability to print in color (if done in house) or pay for color will also play a role in how much it's used. Color can get pretty expensive if a commercial printer is utilized for the production process, which is why I recommend desktop publishing.

Most readers want color in their publications because it's pleasing to the eye, especially color photographs. That wasn't the case 25 years ago when most newspapers and newsletters were printed without color. Today's technology, however, has made it a rarity to see any publication using strictly black and white.

But what about words and other items in newsletters – when should they be printed in color?

Colored fonts should be utilized sparingly – maybe if a quote is pulled out of an article and enlarged. Drop caps (a large first letter of a word at the beginning of the article) will also stand out if they colored. Another time to use a color font might be in a sentence emphasizing a warning or reminder such as, "All employees should be aware that the parking lot will be blacktopped on Monday so alternate parking is required." That can be printed in red while everything else is in black.

Boxes or borders used around a news article should be black. However, it's okay to incorporate a colored background behind the text – either with or without the black line. This is a nice touch but ensure it's about 20 percent of the original color.

Publishing Non-Traditional Newsletters

As an alternative to 8-16 page publications, consider publishing a brief, one-page newsletter that concentrates only on one subject. Unlike their larger cousins, these types of newsletters are published randomly and serve as a method for delivering significant information that cannot wait for the formality of a full-scale newsletter.

As an example, our company was about to enter labor contract negotiations with the union, and we wanted to remind employees that their benefits are some of the best when compared to other companies. So, we developed a newsletter called "Are You Aware?" We used single editions to focus on health benefits, pay, holidays and various other areas we were preparing to negotiate.

We didn't break our rule of staying on one subject and we never allowed a subject to bleed to the back page. There were enough hard copies printed for every employee plus we emailed them to everyone. It turns out that the 'Are You Aware?' newsletters were popular enough that we continued them for the next several years.

Selecting Printing Paper

Another aspect of publishing and communication, which might appear insignificant, is the choice of printer paper. For creating internal products, keep on hand plenty of 8.5 x 11 printer paper, but not the cheap stuff used in copiers; use bright white, 24-pound paper. Also, keep card stock (60 pound) in the arsenal to serve as report covers or to create some type of safety cards. Card paper costs a little more, but it makes for much more pleasing products.

Print newsletters on 11 x 17 paper, and then fold the pages in half so each sheet equals four pages. Like printer paper, purchase bright white 11x17. When designing the newsletter, remember to set up the document so that the pages are correct when they are printed. For an eight-page newsletter, it will appear on the screen in this fashion: pages 8-1, 2-7, 6-3, 4-5. Print pages 8-1 on one side of the paper and 2-7 on the opposite side. Do the same for 6-3 and 4-5. When they are folded, the newsletter will be in sequential order.

Communicating for Results

Communication is more than informing; make it work for you!

Chapter 5

MAKING COMMUNICATION WORK FOR YOU

There's a huge difference between communication methods produced to inform employees and communication techniques fashioned to induce employee reaction. We've already discussed news dissemination products such as newsletters so now let's turn our attention to a second brand of communication called goal-oriented communication.

Goal-oriented communication – or intermittently referred to a solutions-oriented communication – is intended to encourage and persuade co-workers to actively participate in a project or business plan – to galvanize them to be advocates in the company's success rather than bystanders who watch everybody else contribute. It's methodical in nature and is often utilized to accomplish some type of business goal such as increasing revenue or customer base. It requires strategic thinking and the ability to operate with the end in mind.

So, how does this work? Let's use the rest of this chapter to take a comprehensive look at a fictitious business that is trying to cut costs, increase revenue, and improve its competitive position amongst other like businesses in the same company. You, the reader, are appointed the communication manager.

Due to lower product demand associated with a weak economy, all 23 similar businesses in your company have been mandated by the corporate office to reduce their annual operations budget by 30 percent. In your case, that's about $30 million that needs to be cut – some to be slashed immediately but the entire amount within the next three to four years. (That may be a pittance or huge amount depending on your real business.) To make matters worse, the parent company is now strategically reviewing each of its 23 properties to determine other ways to reduce costs. That strategic review may include reducing capacity at some locations or even closing businesses.

Unfortunately, the strategic review indicates that your respective location is ranked 19th out of 23 businesses on your company's cost curve, which isn't a good place to be – the fourth quartile. This essentially means there are 18 other sister businesses more financially successful than yours, and you are now "on watch" and being discussed by bean counters in a not-so-pleasant manner.

Your general manager calls his management team together to break the bad news – the team must figure out a way to cut costs and/or raise revenue to meet the new budgetary mandate. Otherwise, if management can't handle the problem someone from above will do it for you, which is exactly what you're trying to avoid.

As the communicator, you're listening intensively to the discussions and wonder how you can play a role, how you can enter the equation as a *management resource*. Production managers have ideas on improving output and performance but not the time to properly communicate their desires to reach their business goals. And even if they did, they're usually not too well-versed at it. Moreover, managers are often fighting fires rather than being progressive innovators. And this is a big fire that needs quick reaction.

When communication comes into play, management's typical reaction is to inform employees of what is happening – utilizing the stereotypic communication methods of newsletters, memos and email to inform employees about the plant's predicament. That will normally be their only expectation of you – to inform employees that some types of cuts are going to happen. The thinking is, employees will be more supportive of your budget reduction plans as long as they know about it.

There's nothing wrong with these actions – and they are necessary. But, you have a subsequent idea for the communication process – you want to utilize a proactive approach that will persuade employees to contribute to the cause, not just to know about it. This is where goal-oriented or solutions-oriented communication takes center stage. By using this new line of attack, you are about to embark on a journey that will empower employees with the knowledge and courage to save your business – and that requires them to move out of their comfort zone and to become personally involved.

Using the normal communication strategies of informing employees, you are able to state the problem and what needs to happen – cutting $30 million from the budget and getting out of the dangerous fourth quartile. In the meantime, you develop an umbrella goal of moving the business to a better position on the cost curve, which encompasses the acute and immediate objective of saving $30 million in the budget.

Obviously, $30 million is a lot of money and, quite frankly, only a smidgen of the population has any idea how to comprehend having that kind of cash. As the communicator in this exercise, it's not your job to determine where the cuts come from; rather, you have the job of convincing employees to do it.

The initial reaction for reducing budgets is to first cut out the proverbial fat. That might include reducing travel, halt training classes, or initiating a hiring freeze – all of which are considered low hanging fruit or nuisance expenditures that rarely or dramatically affect the current workforce.

So, how will you persuade employees to lend a hand in reducing $30 million from the operations budget and moving the business up the company's cost curve?

Employees will understand the immediate need to save money if the reason why is explained in terms they can comprehend. In other words, give them similar comparisons of saving workplace money to their own challenges of reducing their household expenses by a third. At home, they would look to their own low hanging fruit – no more eating out, no needless travel to the mall, holding off on buying a new car or maybe cancelling a vacation. People can suffer these things for a while, but they have more trouble with getting hit where it hurts: cancelling cable television, stopping cell phone service, cutting off the internet, lowering the thermostat, eating television dinners, drinking water instead of soft drinks or maybe selling their house for something smaller and less expensive. In a dire situation, the communicator must convince employees that their business is at the point of eating macaroni and cheese and Ramen noodles three times a day. That will get their attention.

The trouble is businesses will rarely find enough savings from these cuts to meet their budgetary demands. So, the next step is to reduce capital expenditures and employee salaries or to institute a layoff or partial shutdown of the business.

The smart play in getting employees involved is to do so in a proactive manner. Make it unmistakably clear that 19th place puts the business in danger of falling off the cliff if things get worse. At the same time, saving money and moving to the positive side of the cost curve is possible if everyone works together.

Next, set and state a reasonable and achievable goal for the plant.

For this case, your stated goal will be to move to the 10th position on the company's cost curve. You may ask, "why not shoot for the top five or number one"? First of all, it may be implausible to progress to this point because of underlying issues such as equipment and location problems. More importantly, however, is that the target should be attainable – not too hard, but not too easy, either. We're talking about jobs and livelihoods here, not a basketball tournament.

Finance experts are more concerned with the top 25 percent and the bottom 25 percent of those businesses on the company's cost curve – more so on the struggling plants. They want the top businesses to keep up what they are doing so there's not as much inclination to suggest interfering with what isn't broken. Instead, they direct their trained eyes to the bottom of the heap, which is where you are. Just remember that finance gurus make recommendations based on the bottom line – it's not an emotional experience for them like it is for your employees. If your business needs to cut $30 million, then employees need to accept that in a dispassionate sense.

Keep in mind, too, that while you have to cut your budget by a third, your competition is doing the same thing – and that makes it nearly impossible to move up the cost curve without a more stringent goal. In other words, while you run, they run. So, you need to run faster and employee involvement will get you there – thus, in reality, your business will likely need $40 million in cuts to move up the company cost curve.

With your rallying point (goal) of being 10th on the cost curve adequately stated, it's time to illustrate it visually. A good tool for this is to develop a graph showing where all the businesses are located on the cost curve and an arrow pointing to where your

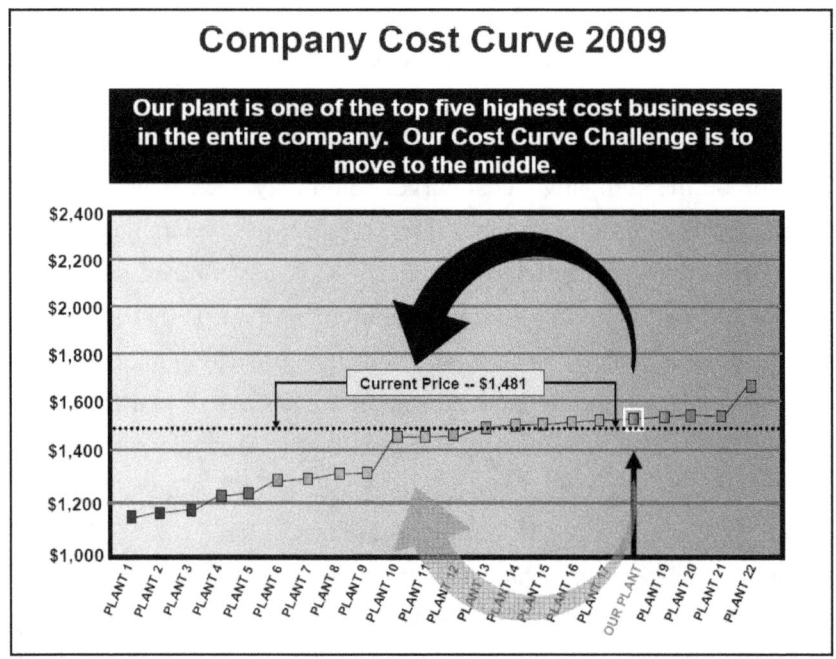

company needs to be situated within a specific timeframe. Add color to the graph showing each of the quartiles and that your business sits in the fourth quartile. The illustration on this page depicts a color gradient with green being excellent, yellow is average, and red is the worst – just like a traffic signal. The deeper the red, the more trouble the plant is in.

Along with the cost curve graph, craft a brief internal news article about the cost curve goal. This is where you accentuate the need for a collective effort of all employees to get your plant out of harms way. Subsequently, make a two or three slide presentation that management can use in their departments. The cost curve itself, admittedly, may contain some apples to oranges comparisons, but the end result is the bottom line doesn't lie to financial experts, which is your primary point here.

The next step is to develop communication strategies to reach the 10th position. The general manager will eventually determine specific actions for cutting costs, so your main priority is develop the "map" to success. This will include:

- Creating a High-Level Cost Curve Roadmap
- Stakeholders' Mapping and Strategies
- High-level Communications Calendar
- Key Performance Indicators
- Dashboards

CREATING A HIGH-LEVEL ROADMAP

Now that your goal is established, the next step is to show employees the way to success. This is the time to develop a visual roadmap that succinctly illustrates to employees where their journey will lead them from beginning to the end. Think of such a roadmap as a one-page, pie in the sky planning tool to reach your goal. It's not intended to replace a business plan.

The roadmap pictured on this page was developed with the cost curve goal in mind – reaching the 10th position on the company's cost curve. While the roadmap may appear to be a document that can be prepared in 30 minutes, it takes much more understanding of your current business landscape before developing it.

An acceptable roadmap will include a timeline to reach a goal – a starting point (2014 in this case) and an end date (2017). For this exercise, let's say your strategic actions will come in "waves" or phases. The first wave of objectives will last about a year, which is the timeframe you've given yourself to save the first $10 million; the second wave (another $10 million) in two years; and the third wave (the final $10 million) will take about a year. Each wave will have its own objectives for saving money. (Just keep in mind that you'll need to squeeze another $10 million 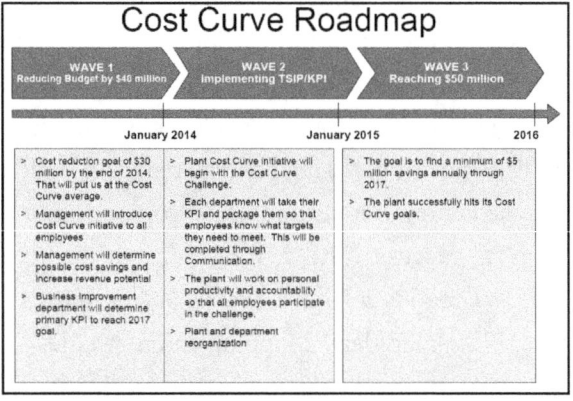 savings in there, too, in hopes of staying ahead of the competition. However, it's best not to be overwhelming, especially during the first year when the original mandate presents quite a shock to employees. Once they begin participating, they'll accept the additional $10 million challenge.)

Next, highlight the actions to be used during each wave and what you expect to occur during that timeframe – maybe 3-5 actions for each wave. The word "highlight" should be emphasized here; the actual strategies will be much more detailed by your management team.

INDENTIFYING AND MAPPING STAKEHOLDERS

Management and the communicator should know where their target audience (stakeholders) is positioned in helping the business reach its cost curve goal. Don't assume everyone backs the endeavor, especially if there is a union where labor leaders and management often disagree on the company's direction, such as a workforce reduction.

With a large amount of stakeholders intertwined in the cost curve goal, it's time to create a Stakeholder Map, sometimes referred to as a stakeholder participation matrix. The map allows management to reserve judgment, at any particular point in time, on where each of their stakeholders stands in terms of helping the business reach its goal. The map on this page – produced and intended only for management – is the first guesstimate on where management thinks stakeholders stand; it will likely be altered in the weeks and months ahead.

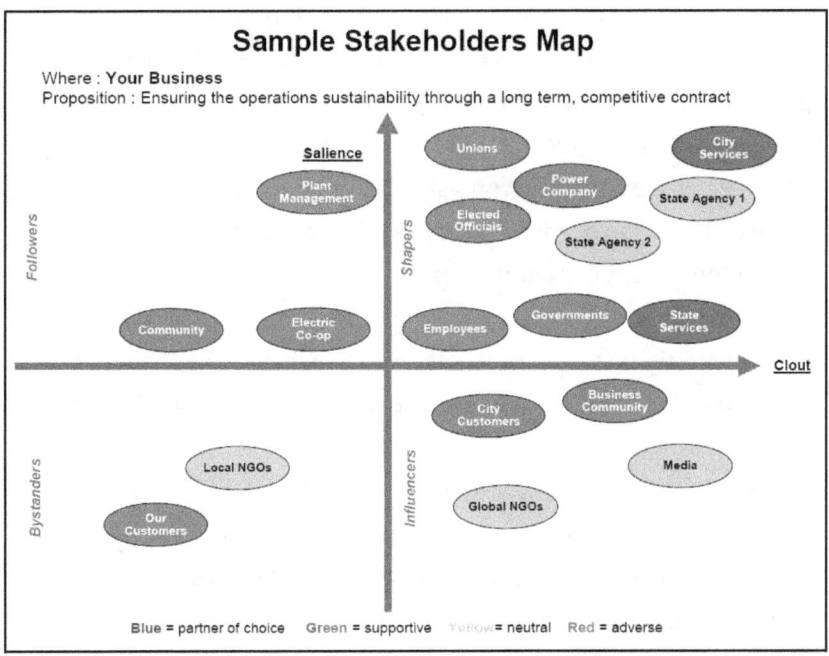

77

Notice all but a couple of the stakeholders are listed in progression of importance to the Cost Curve project. The upper right portion of the map is the "Shapers", those stakeholders who comprise the most influence on your cost curve goals. At the bottom right are the second most influential, then the followers and finally the bystanders.

The green colored circles describe the stakeholders who offer the highest support in reaching the Cost Curve goal. The yellow circles represent groups in 'standby' mode. These groups are undecided at the moment, but could change at any time. Their movement depends on the company's efforts. In red are those groups or entities that are least inclined to support your position. Mapping stakeholders should be decided by more than just one person. In fact, it may be best to have four or five people come to a consensus on each group before assigning a color to it.

With the stakeholders identified, the next objective is to develop strategies for interacting with each of them – most importantly those with the highest influence. How will they react to the goal? Are they opinionated? Do they generally have a respectable attitude on change? Are they agreeable to help you reach the goal? The point to remember is there isn't a "one-size-fits-all" stakeholder engagement strategy. Each one needs to be approached differently.

In this case, your employees are the most significant stakeholder in achieving the cost curve goal. For them, it's all about comprehending the "who, what, where, when, why and how" of having to reduce costs. (You can use tactics identified in the previous chapter.)

With negative stakeholders, it would benefit management to host a meeting with the person(s) to confirm their suspicions as to why they will not help the business achieve its goal. Even though there aren't too many of them, they will require as much attention as those in green. Once it has been determined why they are unsupportive, a decision will need to be made on whether or not their stance can be reversed. If so, the next step is to develop objectives to address their issues.

HIGH-LEVEL COMMUNICATION CALENDAR

A High Level Communications Calendar is an uncomplicated, one-page document developed in Microsoft Word that tracks communication activities related to a project – in this case, the cost curve goal. The intent of this tool is to allow management to list planned action items associated with the goal and to assess the success of each one.

The calendar is formatted so that the months are at the top of the page, and the topics are listed down the left side – somewhat like a grid. Next, type a brief description of the action items you plan to implement corresponding to the topic and the month in which they will be executed. Place a diamond bullet next to each action plan, and color code the diamond to determine whether it is planned, in progress or completed.

Black diamonds mean the action item is scheduled; yellow diamonds means the action is in progress; green indicates the action is complete; and red signifies actions occurred without planning, such as a media report.

The calendar is an ever-evolving practice and will be updated as the days and months pass. It should be evaluated at least once a week, more often if there are several action items occurring.

KEY PERFORMANCE INDICATORS & DASHBOARDS

One way to determine whether the business is meeting its goals and on the pathway to success is to develop a measurement system to quantifiably track the business's progress. The preeminent approach for doing this is to build Key Performance Indicators (KPI). A KPI is a performance measurement component used to show progress toward a specific goal.

For example, a local school system that plans to be the best in the state may assign graduation rates and test scores as their KPI. These two issues need to improve before they can reach their overall goal. A vehicle manufacturer striving to have the best safety performance in the industry may select the number of recalls over the past five years as one of its KPI. Whatever the KPI is selected, it has to be important to the organization's success.

After establishing your KPI, in our case one of them will be the amount of money saved toward $30 million, it's imperative that they are displayed and updated regularly. One way to do that is to create a monthly KPI newsletter for employees. The publication shouldn't be filled with articles; rather, it should have a graph for each KPI and a written synopsis of the month-to-month performance next to the KPI.

While we're on the subject of displaying the KPI, another worthwhile communication tool to consider for the cost curve goal is to create a dashboard. A dashboard is a large visual aid that allows employees to see the overall business goal and how they are progressing towards it.

To get a better idea of what a dashboard might look like, think of a vehicle dashboard with indicators for gasoline, mileage, RPM and speed. The dashboard stays in the driver's vision and is constantly changing as the car pushes toward its destination.

From the cost curve perspective, we know you have a $30 million gap (or savings) to fill in order to move from 19th to 10th on the company's cost curve (remember, it's the $30 million in mandated cuts and the extra $10 million needed to get ahead of the internal competition). So, let's establish a theme for the dashboard you will build – how about "Bridge the Gap" since you certainly have a big one to fill.

The dashboard needs to be large enough for everyone to see, and it should be displayed in a strategic location. As shown in the

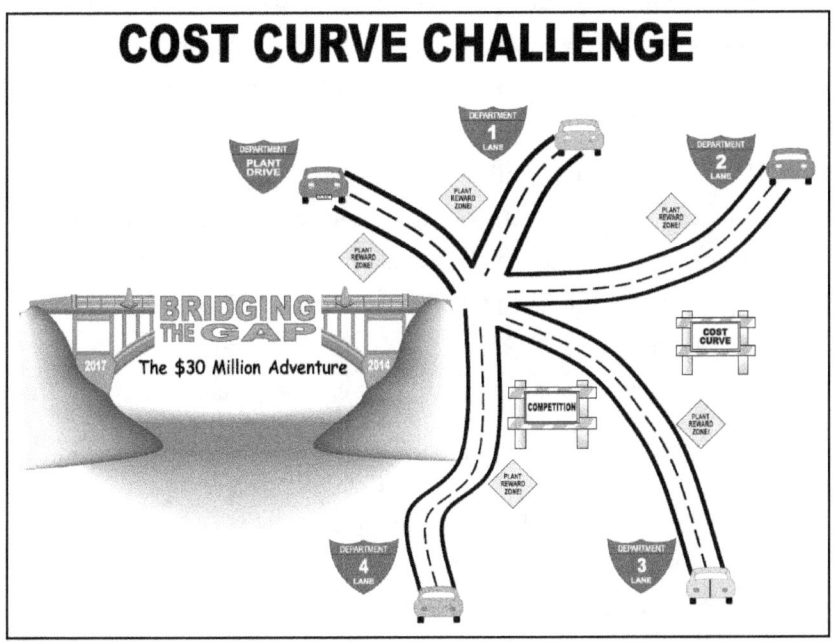

accompanying illustration, design a bridge so that it is half-built between two ends of a road. What you want to do is Bridge the Gap – or start building the bridge – each time your business saves a $1 million. Hire someone to cut out a large metal sign, maybe six feet wide by four feet tall, and have the bridge designed on metal. (By utilizing metal for the dashboard, pieces of the bridge can be made on magnets.)

If there's a bridge, then there has to be vehicles approaching it, right? To gain department involvement, and maybe a little competition, outline roads headed for the bridge for each production area. As each department finds savings, move their respective magnetic car up the road to where it meets the bridge. Obviously, the car can make it to the bridge, but it can't travel across unless the bridge is finished.

Obviously, the objective is to completely finish the bridge. When that is accomplished, have a meal or some other type of attractive incentive for all employees. Plan to keep the Bridge the Gap sign hanging for a few years and, by all means, continue to update it each time the business hits a savings milestone ($1 million in our case).

If hanging a metal billboard isn't an option, another type of dashboard can be displayed through an internal television network. With computers and high end televisions being more compatible, a business can easily create the bridge through a software program and display it on the TV.

Yet another type of dashboard that can be created relatively free is to do so in PowerPoint – a visual that can be shown every time there is a business meeting or gathering of employees.

To keep employees further aligned with the cost curve goal, you may also want to create another graphic showing where the business stands against its 22 sister plants. One idea is to design a conveyor belt (with clipart or photo) showing where everyone stands on the cost curve. The names of the best plants are at the top with the fourth quartile businesses located at the bottom. Obviously, being on the bottom with the threat of falling off speaks volumes for your critical situation.

PowerPoint will allow the user to actually animate the names so they are moving on the conveyor. In fact, the creator can take the name of the business – in the 19th position – and make it transition to the number 10 spot so as to illustrate the cost curve goal. To be more dramatic, list the names of closed businesses on the floor.

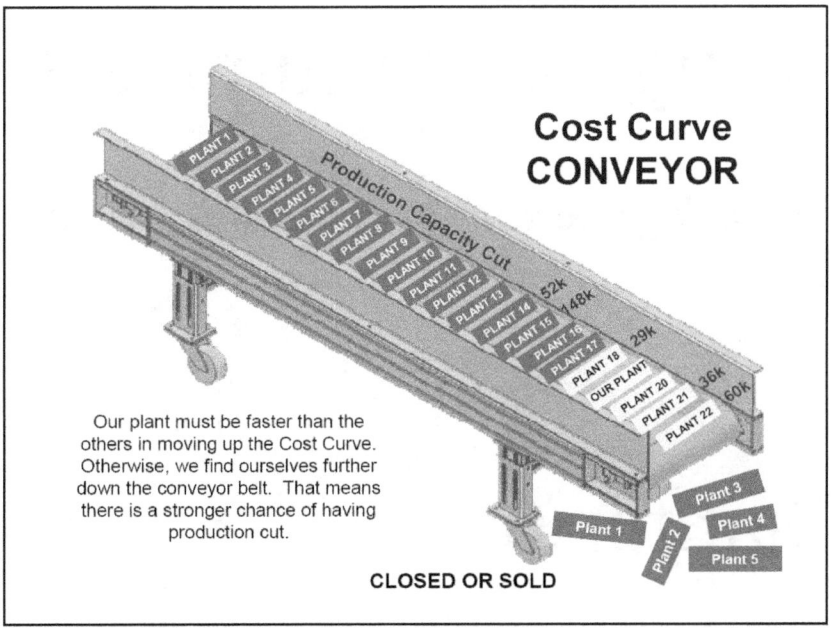

Promoting Safety through Communication

You can't go wrong by developing safety products

Chapter 6

SAFETY: IT'S EVERYBODY'S BUSINESS

The laws of probability say an employee will eventually suffer an injury in some type of accident. Whether it's a simple nick on the finger from a paper cut or a broken arm induced by a fall down the stairwell, an accident will happen at some time or another. Unfortunately, it's usually not until after the accident that the businesses begin promoting safety awareness. In other words, it's a reactionary measure instead of a proactive one.

Communicators who want an instant winner in making communication a part of the business solution should focus on employee safety. It doesn't matter if their company is heavy industrial or a venture with a handful of employees; when safety is promoted, everybody benefits.

To get started down the path of promoting safety, the best place to begin is with the company's safety representative. He or she can provide ideas on what needs to be communicated or, at the very least, lend the communicator a copy of the company's guidelines for responding to injuries. Whether those plans are codified and readily available or if they need to be dusted off and revisited, there are plans stashed somewhere.

Safety personnel are usually very competent in their jobs, whether they are installing safety barricades or sending out an alert email warning employees about traffic dangers. They draft policies, hand out protective equipment, and complete reports for local, state and federal regulators. However, communication presentations and safety promotion isn't their strong suit – which is why the communicator is their knight in shining armor.

So, how can a communicator help improve safety? How can he prevent Cindy or Steve from accidently catching a piece of dust in the eye when he's not on the floor? Well, it could be as simple as working with a safety team to generate an affable reminder about eye injury probabilities. In this case, Steve needs to be aware of how safety glasses are essential personal protection equipment when using an air compressor. And, if Cindy doesn't use machinery at work, maybe she'll use a leaf blower at home and remember the safety tip.

It takes a bit of creative juices to "step outside the box" to promote safety. It also requires some time beyond one's conventional duties. Nevertheless, reducing the danger of employee and visitor injuries is a noble gesture and worthwhile endeavor.

So, let's look at some different avenues for promoting safety.

DESIGNING SAFETY POSTERS

Any workplace where goods are being produced, especially in a manufacturing environment, there's a better than average chance that some form of safety reminders are posted to encourage employees to work safely. Those might include notices printed on copy paper, placards or even large billboards usually purchased from an outside vendor.

They may promote severe weather awareness, environmental consciousness, personal protection equipment or fire safety, just to name a few. They are all fairly decent and serve the purpose for general safety attentiveness. Nevertheless, they are also generic, meaning they are not personalized for a particular business; albeit, one can pay extra to get a company's name and logo printed on them.

Certainly, that's one way to go. However, a business can get more for its money if some of these items are created in-house, like safety posters. These are usually purchased by the safety team and focus on a particular topic like pedestrian traffic or being alert to flu symptoms. These one-size-fits-all posters are okay to use, but this book is about creating items like these on your own terms – to personalize them for your business.

To create safety posters, the first step is to talk with the company's safety representative to determine if there's a particular topic that needs attention. Better yet, maybe there is a wide array of issues that may result in the creation of a campaign. For the purposes of this exercise, let's say we'll commission a safety campaign to include a broad sweep of topics, say maybe 10 posters, each focusing on separate subjects.

Our first step is to establish an unambiguous theme that can be promoted – something short and easy to comprehend. Let's say "Choose Wisely," because we want employees to think before acting, thus being proactive instead of reactive. If they "choose wisely" where safety is concerned, they will end up going home as healthy as they were when they arrived.

Along with theme, let's create a logo that will be printed on all the posters. For our exercise we'll create a logo called, "Safety: Zero In." (The logo can serve dual purposes like being printed on stationary, memos or even bumper stickers.) With the theme name and logo ready to go, it's time to select a topic and design the poster – the fun part of the campaign. By the way, once the type style and logo is selected, stay with it throughout the campaign.

Our first poster will focus on heat stress since employees work around machinery that emits excessive heat. Coupled with hot summer weather, employees need to be aware of heat stress dangers.

The next step is to select the poster's background – what we want it to look like. Since it's about heat stress, we obviously want something related to heat. There are many possibilities such as an employee wiping off sweat, the sun beating down on a desert, or steam rising off equipment – whatever one's imagination comes up with; it just needs to be intriguing. If nothing strikes your fancy, look to the internet for some backgrounds; there are plenty of photographs available for download or purchase.

The background for our heat stress poster (illustrated here) shows a burning match. When I came up with this idea I asked an employee to strike a match while I took continuous photos. I chose the best one and then added some distortion to the background. Whenever the background is chosen, carefully resize, crop and then paste it on the computer's blank page.

Next, compose a short message about the dangers of heat stress – maybe one sentence – that will be printed on the poster. Our message will be: "When the body is unable to cool itself by sweating, several heat-induced illnesses can occur such as heat stress or heat exhaustion."

Then arrange the message, Choose Wisely theme, poster logo, and the company's logo on the page. That's really all is needed to start a poster campaign. If 11x17 isn't large enough, take the digital documents to a local printer and have them print larger sizes.

Once you get started, you'll envision all kinds of posters. The second poster I made was derived after visiting a convenience store one morning and noticed a lottery ticket lying on the ground. When I arrived at work and had some time, I designed a lottery ticket focusing on LOTO – Lock Out, Tag Out.

MOTIVATE EMPLOYEES THROUGH THE BRAVO! PROGRAM

No matter the size of the business, whether it's a small firm with a few employees or a manufacturing facility with hundreds milling around a complex, there are untapped human resources just waiting to be found – people with great ingenuity and ideas on how to make the business better. The big problem is discovering these people.

Employees are oftentimes wary of offering up improvement ideas either for fear of getting turned down; they're too complacent to get involved; or, worse yet, having their ideas ripped off by co-workers or managers. It's crazy to think how many ideas are out there floating around but no avenue in which to express them.

Enter BRAVO!, a safety incentive program aimed at encouraging workers to use their creative juices to correct a safety problem. BRAVO! is somewhat related to any other employee suggestion program that companies and non-profit organizations incorporate with the intention of securing more employee involvement. The big difference, however, is that ideas are only half the requirement with BRAVO! – the other part is to ensure the idea is implemented.

Here's how it works:

Employees can cultivate safety improvement ideas and then complete a one-page suggestion form stating who they are, where they work (department), and their idea. Next, they take the proposal to their supervisor who determines if the associated costs and time are worth sinking into the project. If so, the employee must complete the project, regardless of the amount of time it takes. When it is finished, the manager provides the final signature and an estimated cost savings for the project.

BRAVO!
PROGRAM RULES

WHAT IS THE BRAVO INITIATIVE?
The BRAVO initiative is a new monetary award and employee recognition program that offers workers an opportunity to implement an idea that will improve an area within Environmental, Health and Safety. It's very simple: complete the form on the first page and explain how you changed or added something during the month that has made an impact on one of the areas within EHS. (As an example, you may have created a new tool that is ergonomically better for you and your fellow co-workers.)

All entries will be judged by the management team and one winner will receive $500 and become eligible for a $5,000 award at the end of the year. **YOU MUST IMPLEMENT OR MAKE THE CHANGE BEFORE YOU CAN BE ENTERED INTO THE DRAWING.** A winner will be chosen at the beginning of each month. If your idea is implemented but your name was not drawn, you will receive a certificate of achievement from the plant manager. As a federal requirement, all awards will be taxed as income.

BEFORE MAKING THE CHANGE
Before you make any changes to your area or make any improvements, you must first have the Safety Training and Communication Representative (department safety representative) in your area to evaluate and approve the change.

NEED HELP WITH YOUR IDEA?
Your supervisor is always available—it's still your suggestion and you will get full credit. Your leader may be able to assist you in implementing your idea.

HOW TO COMPLETE YOUR SUGGESTION

1. Type or print the required information in the spaces on the form. Illegible suggestions will be returned. (Your entry must reproduce on copy equipment.)
2. Use a separate form for each entry. You may enter several changes and they will be judged separately.
3. Indicate whether your idea affects a single department or multiple departments.
4. Give a short title that you think best describes the change you made.
5. Explain how the EHS issue was (if it already existed). In other words, tell what the problem was before you fixed it.
6. Describe the advantages now that you've changed it.
7. Attach photos of the before and after. You may use a blank sheet to attach the photos or you can use the space on the front of the application.
8. Sign the form in the proper space. If there is more than one employee (a team) each person should sign the form and other identifying information. Multiple winners from one entry will share the monthly award as well as the annual award if they are chosen as the top entry for the year.

GOOD LUCK AND THANK YOU FOR PARTICIPATING!

The project is then entered into a monthly drawing against other employees who completed other BRAVO! projects. At the end of the month, the management team carefully examines each submission and picks the one making the biggest impact. The winner receives $500. Employees who do not win the monthly prize receive a gift card from a local restaurant plus they receive a certificate of achievement.

All 12 monthly winners are then entered into a year-end drawing for a chance to win $5,000. When the time arrives for the annual award, arrange a catered luncheon for all monthly winners and the management team. It is there when the annual winner is named.

Keep in mind that some manufacturing facilities spend hundreds of thousands of dollars each year for safety programs and improvements, so $11,000 (12 $500 awards and one $5,000 annual award) is a drop in the bucket and worth a try. You might be incredibly surprised at the results.

One particular business used BRAVO! and averaged six completed projects each month, most of which saved the plant thousands of dollars and/or helped lower safety hazards that could end up costing many more thousands in medical and workers compensation costs. Their annual BRAVO! budget was earned back in one month. In fact, this location saved close to $250,000 the first year alone.

BUILDING A CRISIS COMMUNICATION PLAN

In business and industrial settings, a crisis can arise with little or no advance warning – whether it is an explosion, environmental disaster, weather emergency, or workplace violence. When it does occur, it's a good bet that panic will be the order of the day.

Managers, safety and security personnel will spring into action, most likely following their own guidelines on how to deal with the event. The communicator will also become an integral part of the process since communication will become the hottest commodity. Employees and family members will want to know what's going on and whether the all-clear sign is given.

Not only will the communicator be in charge of developing and disseminating messages to co-workers, overly aggressive journalists may be knocking down the door. Needless to say, orderly and accurate communication becomes obligatory. Thus, it's a good idea for the communicator to be proactive and develop his or her own crisis communication plan to help guide them through critical situations – a much needed crutch to lean on.

A crisis communication plan can be drafted to be prescriptive – one that offers step by step instructions on how to react to these events. Another type of plan includes documents and guidelines one can refer to during the day. Either one, when building a crisis communication plan, here are some documents to consider for inclusion:

- Example(s) of a crisis condition that might occur – maybe a chemical spill or structure fire. This will include a few paragraphs about what a possible event might look like.
- Communication roles during a crisis: identifying who is responsible for receiving media inquiries – the appointed spokesperson; the safety or security officer in command; and the person who will guide the media to a specific location when they arrive.
- Establishing a temporary media center. The last thing a communicator wants is for the media to arrive and walk in the front door with cameras rolling. Even worse, some media will totally disregard visitor protocol and get loose on the property. For this reason, a certain building or conference room needs to be designated for reporters to receive press

releases or verbal updates. Don't turn away reporters; just ask them to be respectful and orderly.

- Include a news release template where the communicator can fill in the blanks.
- Spokesperson roles – how he or she addresses the media.
- A leadership list – those people assigned to deal with the emergency (crisis communication team members).
- Updated company information documents such as an economic impact report showing the company's importance to the community. Include a company background sheet – with information about the items produced, number of employees, safety records, environmental commitment...etc. These should be ready to be copied and provided to the media. Here is a tip: do not depend solely on digital documents because a power outage may keep them from being pulled up on the computer.
- An internal crisis communication contact list, which is different from the leadership list. It's unlikely that the communicator will have exclusive understanding about the disaster so it's imperative someone in the organization can talk rationally and with expertise in relation to the incident. As an example, an environmental reporter may want to know the exact contents and reactions of any spilled material. The environmental manager should be the contact.
- Names and phone numbers of all emergency personnel and management.
- List of organizations and stakeholders, including their telephone numbers. This list could contain several dozen people, depending on the town's size. As an example, the list may contain area emergency services dispatch, fire departments (city, county, volunteer), police departments,

health department, ambulance services, weather service, Coast Guard, electric utilities…etc.
- Local media contacts: Direct phone numbers, email addresses, fax machine numbers and mailing addresses of all newspapers, radio and television stations and reporters.
- Government contacts: including all information for local elected officials at the city, county, state and federal levels.
- A contact log. This is used to record the date and time media representatives call, their company affiliation, and the information they requested. Above all, do not forget to return their phone calls.
- Crisis occurrence documentation list. As the business reacts to the crisis, jot down the company's specific actions – the exact times and a summary of how emergency personnel reacted. For instance, if an employee is sent to the hospital, document it. If personnel extinguish a fire, write it down. This is done to preserve a permanent record that can be referred to once the event is under control.
- A response effectiveness audit: when everything is complete, audit the communication responses to verify whether the team's efforts were ineffective, effective or very effective. This will help improve performance if another disaster strikes.

The length of such a crisis communication plan may be 25 pages long. That might appear somewhat lengthy but remember it contains materials that can be copied and distributed to the media.

Once the plan is completed, review it at least annually to keep the information updated.

EMERGENCY QUICK REFERENCE GUIDE

After creating the crisis communication plan, let's now develop a tool to help employees know what to do during an emergency situation. It's called, no drum roll required, an Emergency Procedures Quick Reference Guide. The guide includes 5-10 pages of instruction for responding to an emergency – sort of a "who, what, where, when and why" handbook.

Like unexpected employee injuries, there's usually little or no warning before an emergency occurs. When it does, we sometimes react irrationally – and that can cause even more heartache. Creating

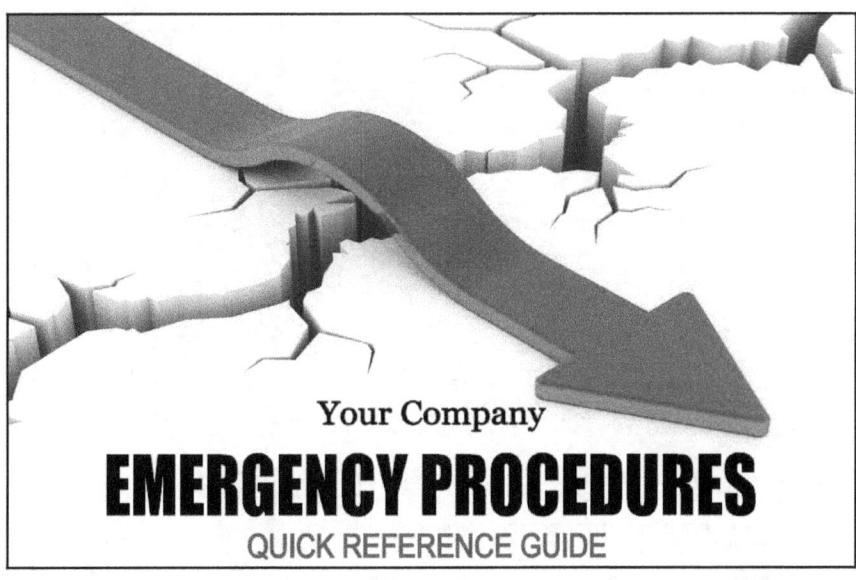

EMERGENCY TELEPHONE NUMBERS

FIRE EMERGENCY

INJURY AND ILLNESS

HAZARDOUS MATERIALS SPILL

MUSTER STATION LISTING

SEVERE WEATHER ALERTS

SEVERE WEATHER SHELTER LISTING

a reference guide for employees to follow doesn't guarantee they will respond properly, but it can give them a foundation in which to try.

A quick reference guide can be developed entirely at the workplace by utilizing desktop publishing techniques. We'll get to the list of documents to include in a moment, but let's first envision how the product will look.

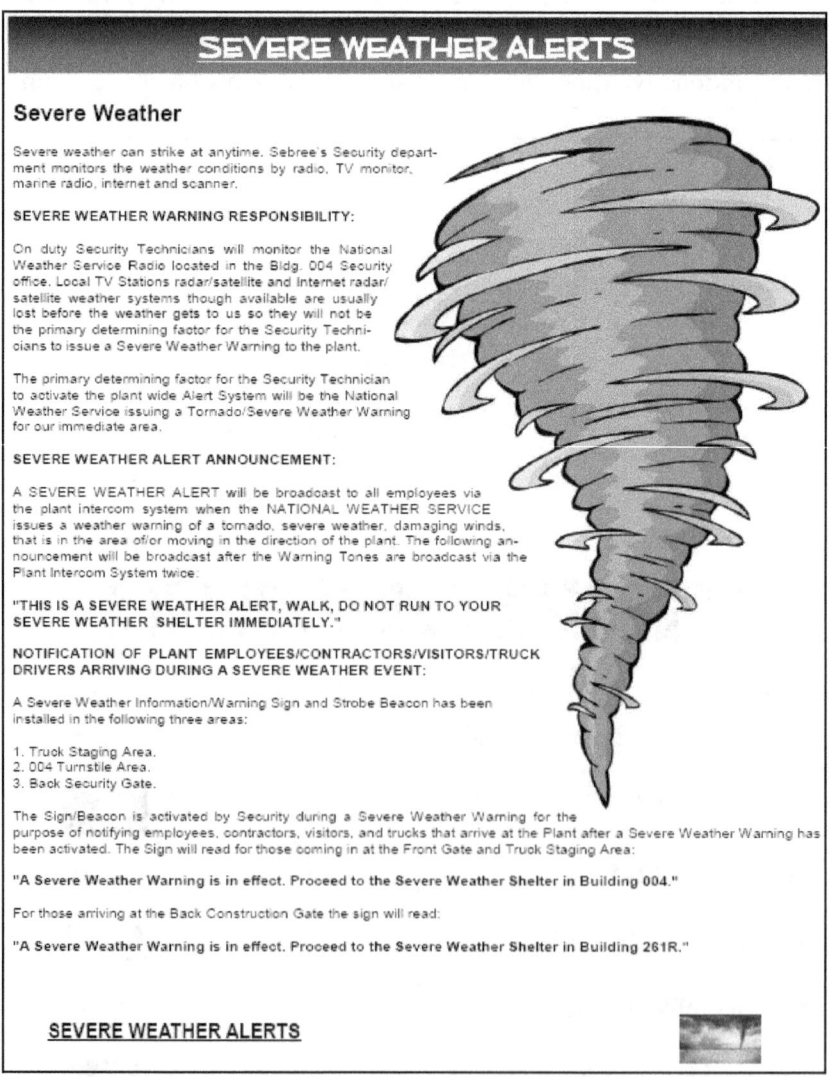

Imagine a common wall calendar, one that has a picture at the top and the month outlined at the bottom. When the month is over, flip the page up, place a stickpin through the hole, and a new month begins. For our quick reference guide, we'll use a similar technique, but ours will be bound by a plastic spiral binder instead of staples – we want ours to look better. As for the paper, we'll choose to print our guide on card stock paper (60-pound) instead of using slick, thin paper like a wall calendar.

Another variation that we'll incorporate is to cut each preceding page one-half inch shorter than the next. For example, the cover page is 8.5 x 8 inches; the second page is a half-inch longer; the third page another half-inch longer; and so on. The final page is 8.5 x 11 (or shorter, depending on the amount of subjects). The length variances allow the titles of each section to be printed at the bottom of their respective pages. All the pages will be printed on full-length paper, but we'll chop off the unused parts with a table cutter.

The cover can be designed in whatever manner is best for the business. The inside pages may be formatted to include the following:

1. Emergency Telephone Numbers (8.5 x 8): for emergency personnel – both inside and out.
2. Fire Emergency (8.5 x 8.5): It has a set of guidelines on what to do during fires – like knowing the type of fire extinguisher to use on different blazes. Also list telephone numbers that employees can call to summon help.
3. Injury and Illness (8.5 x 9): Includes phone numbers in case there is an injury or someone reports a serious illness.
4. Hazardous Materials Spill (8.5 x 9.5): Includes examples of spills and the appropriate steps to take to report a spill.
5. Muster Station Listing (8.5 x 10): Includes all locations where employees should meet and be accounted for after an emergency is over.

6. Severe Weather Alerts (8.5 x 10.5): What to do if a weather watch or warning is issued.
7. Severe Weather Shelter Listing (8.5 x 11): Where to go in case a severe weather emergency occurs.

Special design software is not needed to make the guide – it can be created in Microsoft Word. To print 250 reference guides, it takes an hour or so to cut all the pages and a few more hours to bind them with the spiral binder. It's a full day's project, with design, printing and all.

Who knows, maybe a life can be saved with this practice.

OTHER SAFETY COMMUNICATION IDEAS

The possibilities are endless for improving safety through communication efforts, but here are some more ideas:

- Every time a meeting begins, ask an employee to give a brief 1-2 minute safety message. It can be about something that happened to them – say a near miss accident at work or at home. If severe weather is expected, this would be a good time to remind everyone.
- Place an advertisement in the local newspaper promoting safety.
- Establish and post a safety mission statement in which management endorses and signs.
- Dedicate a specific spot on the company's intranet or internet page for safety messages and activities.
- Host a public safety group meeting at work. As an example, if the community has an emergency management agency where its members meet once a month or every quarter, invite them to hold the meeting at your workplace. Provide them with lunch and refreshments.

- Publish a safety handbook containing all of the company's safety policies. (By the way, this is a perfect opportunity to eradicate outdated policies.)

External Communication Practices

Learning to build your company's reputation

Chapter 7

At some point, a business will reach out for community support. It might be to ask residents to oppose a new state tax which could result in a tremendous cost to the company. Maybe it is applying for a federal grant to help fund a new project and approval is required from elected officials. Or, maybe the company made a big environmental gaffe and is pleading for forgiveness. Asking for community support isn't as easy as it sounds, especially if the company lacks the prerequisites of being upstanding corporate citizen.

It generally takes years to build a strong reputation in the community; companies aren't bestowed with this honor without doing

some work up front. Donating $5,000 to a non-profit organization and then declaring themselves as a responsible corporate citizen doesn't cut it. A business must spend time getting to know the community and vice versa.

Here's another way to look at it – from the marriage perspective. If a husband wants a big ticket item, say a sports car or the chance to go on a golfing trip with his friends, it might take a bit of schmoozing with the wife before she gives her hubby the blessing to move forward. That might include taking on extra jobs around the house, giving her back rubs, or promising her she can go somewhere with the girls. In short, the husband is building up a credit of goodwill that he will soon try to use. It's no different for a business trying to gain favorable status in the community.

This chapter includes methods and products communicators can use to build a nice reputation – not just advice on throwing money at non-profit organizations. The public likes creativity and a chance to get to know the company – those are the building blocks for establishing a community partnership.

But before we explore practices a company might use to increase its community awareness, the first order of business is to concentrate on what matters most: employees.

EMPLOYEES ARE PUBLIC RELATIONS ACTIVISTS

The most important and inexpensive public relations tools that companies have at their disposal are employees. They are better than any lobbyist, printed materials, or website that can be purchased to promote the company. Here's why: if an employee speaks highly of his or her workplace then that positive reinforcement will reverberate with the public and last much longer than anything else that can be conceived. People are attracted to positive behavior and for them to hear employees talk favorably about their employer is a strong indicator the company is valued – and that translates to the outside. Long-term loyalty is not something one can buy.

Expecting workers to sign on as company advocates depends exclusively on how they are treated. It's not about how much money they make or the type of health insurance they receive. It's about respect, plain and simple; if they get it, they will return it. And respect begins and ends with communication.

When employees are adequately informed about work-related community activities – they will stand behind management in times of need. Let's take this mock project for example: Say a company is proposing to build a new facility somewhere in town – a move expected to increase employment. The problem is, the company needs zoning approval for the new site, and it just so happens that just down the road a new subdivision recently opened and new houses are being built. There is a chance that city officials may deny the rezoning request because home owners in the subdivision are wary of any noise or pollution that might come from the plant.

The first step toward getting public approval is to openly share with employees what the company plans to do – not send out a press release or share the idea with the Lions Club. Employees should be the first to know so when the time comes to make a public announcement, they can speak intelligently about the project with the neighbors down the street or with friends.

Next, write an elevator speech – a short, concise message containing the 5Ws and H – regarding the company's intentions to expand and the possible hurdles it might face. Then bring together a group of respected employees for an informational session regarding the project. This is the test group. Explain that they are among the first to know and that all other employees will learn the same thing tomorrow. During the session, generate a Question and Answer list of as many Q&A as possible. This part is essential because their questions will reflect what other employees will ask. Then, write a one-page fact sheet for employees, stating the issue at hand, the effects, and the benefits to the company and community. Include contact information so someone with questions can call a manager.

The next day, share the elevator speech with all employees. If time is not critical, recruit one person, say the general manager, to deliver the same message to all employees. Make sure that person is armed with the Q & A.

The messenger should emphasize that neighbors or friends will approach them asking about the project and if they have any questions at all, now is the time to ask them. The following day is when the company makes it public.

There are several reasons why employee should know first; two of the most relevant is to avoid bad blood at the workplace and, second, because the company needs co-workers to be the unofficial spokespersons in their community. By saying "bad blood", this is referring to the fact that employees will be irritated to learn something about their workplace from the media or a neighbor before management tells them.

However, there are some exceptions to the rule. For example, there are regulations and guidelines related to publically traded companies who wish to make announcements about their business – specifically from the financial perspective. If they are buying a company or selling a part of their own, word typically gets out to the media just minutes before everyone else is informed. That way they can avoid insider trading matters.

Outside this condition, give employees the respect they deserve and talk to them first. This will open the floodgate to positive behavior and give the company a leg up from the public relations perspective.

GIVING CREDIT TO GET CREDIT

Participating in external relations activities, such as sponsoring special events or serving on non-profit boards, is a critical business component for companies expecting to earn the title of magnanimous corporate neighbor. Politicians know more about this practice than anybody. When running for office, they roam the neighborhoods and "press the flesh" to increase their odds of getting elected. They participate in public forums and volunteer for non-profit work to show they care – and most of the time it's genuine. What they want in return is to be rewarded on election night.

If elected, their term in office is spent rebuilding their goodwill account by getting area projects approved or helping constituents with civic issues like road repairs. This is their job as elected officials but they also know these good deeds build support for the next election.

Smart business owners and managers also recognize the value of useful public relations, particularly if they have a product to sell. They can often be found attending non-profit meetings or donating products and money to various causes. Some buy advertisements to publicize the company's value while others use the social media route to promote their business. It's all about keeping the company's name visible – positive public relations. And that's what it's all about, right?

Well, that's one way.

Allow me to offer another tactic that will score a company more robust goodwill points than self-promotion: it's called, Give Credit to Get Credit. This is not a plot, ploy or program; it's the practice of encouraging others to promote the company's benevolence and value to the community without asking them. In other words, let others do the bragging for you. This, ladies and gentlemen, is skillful public relations.

Let's say a company is on the verge of spending a few thousand bucks on radio advertisements to promote the company's name – nothing special, just an advertisement campaign. Instead of buying radio spots specifically for the company, how about donating the ad time to a non-profit organization in the company's name?

This is a win/win to the second power for the company! Here's why: the non-profit gets free time to promote itself – something it usually can't afford to do. In return, the company receives a tag line at the end of the advertisement that says something on the order of, "This advertisement is brought to you by…"

The double win occurs because the company still gets mentioned, which is in relation to why the ad was purchased in the first place. Second, listeners (or readers, if it is a newspaper ad) will hear that the company paid for the spot, which they will quickly translate to the company performing a community service. And, that does not take into account the admiration and positive talk the company receives from the non-profit's members.

Here's another idea that might seem obvious: anytime the business receives public praise for a completed a project or external activity, deflect the accommodations to somebody outside the company, even if their role is a minor one. What happens next is the recipient will brag about the company's success just because they were mentioned. Feed the fly with honey is another way of looking at it.

NASCAR drivers are the best examples of this philosophy. It's rare to hear a driver say "I" when discussing a finished race – it is always "we" or the "team" ran efficiently. The drivers will accept the criticism on behalf of the team, or will blame themselves, but not often will they take full credit for a win. They know better. The same can be said for a quarterback who recognizes his offensive line for protecting him. If he doesn't, the next Sunday he might find a clear path is open for an opposing linebacker to smash him into the ground.

Offering credit to others confers upon them a sense of belonging and ownership in a completed project. It empowers them to do more because they know they are appreciated. This is the epitome of Giving Credit to Get Credit.

CONTRIBUTING TO NON-PROFIT GROUPS

Most businesses will set aside a few dollars in their annual budget to donate to non-profit activities. By saying "a few dollars" that can be an amount from $100 to well over $1 million – depending upon the size of the business or corporation. Some businesses give anywhere from one tenth of 1 percent of the previous year's profits to much more than 1 percent.

Regardless of the amount of money the company contributes, the reason they give it is to get some type of recognition in return for their kindness – to build the goodwill account. To be blunt, funds or material are donated not just to be a conscientious corporate neighbor but to get something in return – positive publicity. This may sound rather boorish to some – and they would rather not admit it – but quid pro quo is the prevailing motivation.

Companies need to be selective when donating money, goods or services to non-profit organizations. First, they need validation that the organizations being funded are using the contributions in accordance with their charter. There are many examples of organizations taking donations and then using the money for something other than their intended purpose. Another factor for distributing money is to be fair in who receives it.

Before disseminating contributions, consider these criteria first:
- What city or community do the majority of employees reside?
- To what city or county does the company owe taxes?
- Which organizations maintain the best reputations?
- What groups are highly dependent on charitable donations?
- Determine which groups are not served by the United Way. Try not to double dip by giving to the United Way, who also

happens to fund an organization in which the company might donate to individually.

- Consider organizations employees are involved in. Moreover, if money is donated to an employee's organization, allow him or her to present the company's check – it makes him feel more connected to the operation.
- Are there organizations that treasure the same type of values as yours? For example, safety is a leading priority for industrials so they may target non-profits who focus on safety, like an emergency management agency.
- What organizations do upper management members belong to?
- Maintain the ability to arbitrarily donate dollars to smaller groups like Little League baseball teams and soccer organizations.

The competition for the company's dollars may get fierce – and certainly political. To counter the problem, craft a contribution form for organizations to complete before they can be considered for funding. On the form, have the applicants provide their identification, tax exempt number and what they plan to do with the donation. Don't make it more than two pages, preferably just one page.

The form can be a deterrent for some because there are plenty of people who are just too apathetic to complete it; if that's the case, then they really don't need the money anyway – or they need a new leader. Independently, the form will also allow the company to codify the requests and approvals.

No matter the size of donation, a company representative should write a brief letter to the organization letting them know "Company X" is happy to sponsor their group, and then attach it to the check. Do this on letterhead and sign it in blue ink. (This may sound picky, but recipients can quickly distinguish blue ink from what might appear to be a photocopy.)

If the contribution amount is more significant, schedule a time when the organization's leader can come to the business for a formal presentation – or maybe present the check at their site. Either way, a bit of pomp and circumstance such as a luncheon, brief speech by the manager and a photograph session goes a long way.

For assessment purposes, create a spreadsheet highlighting the organizations who request money, when they requested it, whom the company gives money to, and the employee who was involved with the organization (if any). Be disciplined in recording this data on a weekly basis; otherwise, it can become a cumbersome task if one waits five or six months. At the end of the year, generate a summary of contributions and present it to the general manager, so he or she can see where the money is going – and to know you are keeping a close watch on donations.

ANNUAL COMMUNITY REPORT

To promote a business to a wide audience consider publishing an annual report that can be inserted into local newspapers. Annual reports of this nature are tabloid or booklet sized communication vehicles usually containing information about the company's legacy, community involvement and what it produces.

(Note: This is in no relation to company-produced annual reports aimed at keeping shareholders up-to-date about the previous year's finances.)

Annual reports, sometimes called community or sustainability reports, are valuable because they allow the company to tell its story without having it edited by the newspaper. Plus, the person overseeing the project can decide the type of information going in it and the day it will be inserted into the newspaper. It can be time-consuming to complete but well worth the effort.

A readable and enticing report should be four to eight pages in length, including the front cover. If it's longer than that, then you risk "skimming" – the readers' fine art of opening a few pages and glancing around without actually reading the content. And, by all means, write short articles and incorporate plenty of graphics – in this case, photographs. Keep the information cheerful and ensure the public of the company's stability because that's what they – and your employees – want to see. Here is an annual report content example:

Page 2: Brief message from the general manager

Page 3: Business overview – how long it has operated and the products produced?

Page 4: Community Involvement – list organizations that employees are involved in and/or who the company donates to

Page 5: Community Involvement – include a letter from a non-profit director telling how important the company is to the community

Page 6: Importance to the local, regional, and state economies (economic summary)

Page 7: A letter from the president of the local economic development corporation telling the company's importance to the community

Page 8: Include another testimonial letter – maybe one from an employee. Also, incorporate a story about an employee – maybe someone who invented a new product or worker who has 25-30 years experience.

Every page should include employee photos at work or play, including participating in fundraisers for local non-profit groups. The public knows the business is there to make a product, but they also should see the human side. To take this a step further, send the message that the business is a marvelous place to be employed.

If a non-profit organization is considering publishing an annual report, include articles and photographs from the businesses that helped it survive. To pay for the insert, consider soliciting advertisements from some of the larger firms who support the organization.

SOMETHING FOR THE KIDS: A COLORING BOOK

If the company is looking for an instant win in the public relations realm – and if the communicator is willing to put on his or her artistic hat – here's an idea that is just as much fun to produce as it is effective in building a positive public perception: create a coloring book for children and giving it away to schools.

Before starting this venture, there needs to be a reason why to publish one. The first coloring book I assembled occurred while working for a non-profit education program. Our organization was created to provide elementary through high school students with information about career choices.

For young children, grades K-3, learning about careers was more about awareness of the different types of jobs out there. As they got older, they learned about the particulars of certain jobs, culminating in internships at local businesses while in high school.

To strengthen career awareness for the little kids, an assistant and I chose to create a coloring book that would feature varying jobs of interest – some they are familiar with like police officers, doctors and teachers. To make it more user friendly, we designed a special character who would introduce each career. The character we decided upon was a large apple named Andy – along with his sidekick, Wooly Worm. It was these guys who would guide kids from career (page) to career (page).

We began scanning numerous clip art books to find jobs that we could incorporate the characters into. At the bottom of each page we included a one sentence introduction of the career.

While developing the coloring book, we contacted a dressmaker to assemble a costume character of Andy and Wooly – similar to a Disney costume – which a person could fit inside. The costume was crafted so that a person could stick his/her arm through the worm to make it appear alive. It was not easy to use, and it was warm inside, but it looked absolutely groovy.

We also developed instructional materials that teachers could use to coach children about careers. We solicited help from five first-grade teachers, from five different elementary schools, to write and assess the material. In return, we paid them a small stipend.

After a full three months of working on this package, it was finally done. Promotional flyers about Andy Apple and Wooly Worm were created and sent to every elementary school in the area. Within a week we had booked five appearances.

At each location, we packed the necessary number of coloring books, crayons, rulers and, of course, the apple costume. We moved from room to room handing out the items, which the kids absolutely loved. The amount of hugs and well wishes we received from the kids and teachers was overwhelming.

Seven years later, while working for a local company, I revived the coloring book idea, but with a different purpose. Our company had become concerned that employees were not choosing a healthy lifestyle. This presumption became fact when we held an employee health fair and learned that an alarming number of workers had high cholesterol, smoked and were overweight.

From that point forward, we began hosting wellness classes for our employees and also hired a part-time health coach. During one of the classes, an employee mentioned that he would have liked to known more about healthy choices when he was a kid.

Viola! The idea was sparked for resurrecting the coloring book project.

Similar to the first coloring book, two of us spent time developing a character, resembling an aluminum can, since the company we worked for produced aluminum. His name was "ICAN" and it was his job to teach kids about the importance of healthy eating habits and wellness exercises. This was accomplished through a program I entitled "Healthy Choices".

Instead of creating a character costume or teaching materials, it was our wellness coordinator who attended schools to talk about Healthy Choices – eating right, exercising, and personal hygiene. This time the package included more tangibles: a brown bag with

Some people like to try roller skating
(Activity: Draw a "Please Stay off the Grass" sign near the road)

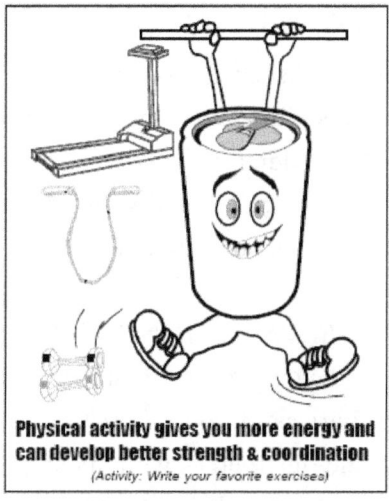

Physical activity gives you more energy and can develop better strength & coordination
(Activity: Write your favorite exercises)

Maybe you can see yourself reading a good book
(Activity: Write the titles of your favorite books on the shelf)

Use lotion when you play in the sun
(Activity: Draw a sand castle in the sand for ICAN)

handles (to promote the environment); pencils that change colors when they are held; a wooden ruler, crayons, and the coloring book.

The teachers loved it, especially because our wellness coordinator reinforced some of the personal hygiene issues like brushing teeth, taking baths…etc. It was her hope that getting people to start healthy habits at a young age would carry over into their adult life.

The entire package didn't cost the school anything – it was all paid for by the company. A local newspaper got wind of our program and published a front-page story on what we were doing for the schools – it was a wonderful public relations piece. As a bonus, some of the children we talked to had parents who worked at our business. It was especially gratifying when the employees mentioned their child took part in our program.

ESTABLISHING AN INTERNET SITE

Knowing how to surf the World Wide Web and understanding the intricate details of creating a website are entirely different aspects of the internet – with most people abstaining from the website building part. It is no wonder why the general public once refrained from producing internet sites because a decade ago it required knowledge of complicated computer codes and HTML language.

Fast forward 10 years and there have been dramatic changes in the computer world as many local businesses and individuals are creating their own websites either to promote a product or to express personal viewpoints about anything from politics to television episodes.

So what changed?

Primarily, we can thank the software industry and their employees for making the task more user-friendly. It no longer takes a college degree in computer programming to set up a website. Now, anybody can do it with a just a few bucks and some online direction. It really is simple.

There are essentially two ways to construct an internet page for a business: 1) hire an outside firm to do it – sometimes at a prohibitive cost – or 2) do it yourself with the help of an internet company. The latter is the best way if the company is looking to save money, in addition to having full control of the website.

(A cautionary comment: there are obvious variations between creating a simple website on your own compared to those produced by professionals – it really depends on the target audience and whether the company is striving for worldwide interest or selling a product.)

The secret to building a low-cost internet site is to utilize an established domain registration and hosting company that has a web page development package available. Two of the more popular domain companies with such offerings are Register.com and GoDaddy.com. If those two don't satisfy one's itch, merely type "domain registration" in a favorite search engine and see what comes up. Regardless of who is chosen, a person can build and maintain a website for less than $200 and then continue administering it for roughly the same amount each year.

The first item of business in creating an internet web page – after management endorsement, of course, is to decide the domain name and whether it is actually available for purchase. In all likelihood if the name of the business is XYZSupport, then the domain, "XYZSupport.com" is the choice. By visiting a domain registration site such as Register.com or Godaddy.com, one can type in the domain and see if it's available – meaning no one else has purchased the same name. If it's available, buy it quickly instead of waiting days or weeks. It initially costs $10-$25 and then about $15 annually to keep it.

Once the domain name is secured, the next step is to purchase the web building package. It will provide step-by-step instructions on how to assemble the front page and every page thereafter. One can choose the shape of the website (vertical or horizontal) add photographs, graphics, hit counter, menus, upload documents, clocks, weather and a host of other add-ons. A traffic analysis package is also available so that the business can see where the hits (visitors) are originating. Without question, a website can be up and functioning in a day.

As for building the website, here are some "dos and don'ts" to consider:

- Don't use music in the background. This is very irritating, and the chances are that the song picked will not be liked by the audience. Even instrumental music can be annoying.
- Animated clip art is okay, but it's probably better not to have it. However, if the site's creator goes this route, use very little of it and don't choose some free, chintzy animated .gif from an obscure website.
- Photos are good, especially if the site is built to be primarily informational. Employees like to see each other and putting them on the web might be considered an honor.
- Choose reader friendly backgrounds for text – probably white. Sites that use a green or blue background and white lettering are taxing on the eyes; absolutely use black text.
- Include privacy and copyright statements.
- Make all links in one color – preferably blue and underlined. This is what people are used to seeing.
- In the navigation bar, there should be a page for "careers" that visitors can click on to see if there are any job openings. Even if the company's isn't hiring, it can at least say that. Also, have an "about us" and "our products" pages.

- Include a page with the website administrator's contact information – or at least an email link if visitors want to leave a message. Along those lines, consider adding a form that visitors can fill out and submit if they want to be contacted. One never knows what that may lead to.
- When posting articles consider putting the most important information at the top, then to the right, the bottom and then the left. This is easier to do if you imagine a reverse "6" on your page.

STARTING A VISITOR AMBASSADOR PROGRAM

There's nothing more gratifying in the human resource profession than to see business clients, customers or guests leave the workplace with a genuine smile on their face, particularly those persons who are influential in the community, region or state. If they can depart with good feelings, the odds greatly improve that the company just made a deposit in the all-important community goodwill account.

Here is another idea to help boost that deposit – and it costs hardly anything:

The next time a distinguished person visits, and before he or she leaves, present him with a certificate naming him a "Company" Ambassador. It's on the same line as distinguishing someone with an honorary degree from a university. While being a company ambassador isn't as prestigious as an honorary degree, it can set your business apart from others who, more than likely, give the person a handshake goodbye.

Earning the ambassadorship depends on many factors – certainly, and most important – the value of conversations and business dealings. It needs to be a quasi-exclusive club, so the distinction is to be handed out sparingly.

The certificate created can be as simple as an 8.5 x 11 card stock or something on a fancier 11 x 17 paper that actually looks like membership certificate. Keep plenty of certificates on hand and use calligraphy (or font) to print the person's name on it. Or, use a computer program and print them when needed.

WRITE SPEECHES TO INFORM

How many luncheons and formal dinners have you been forced to sit through to hear a painstakingly monotonous, uninteresting, twenty-minute soliloquy of blather that some poor sap spent hours writing the day before? Even worse, what about having to listen to it after lunch in a warm room? Jiminy Crickets! It can be torture! Unfortunately, this type of speech happens more often than the sort that puts an audience on the edge of its seat.

The usual dividing line between a boring and riveting speech is dependent upon two key elements: the content and delivery. If the content is interesting, then the audience can withstand a dry delivery. On the other hand, if the person speaking is entertaining, he can compensate for not having an in-depth speech. The best speeches are those that combine useful content and an interesting delivery.

For the purpose of this part of the chapter, let's look at both sides of the equation, with content being first.

Writing the Speech

Preferably, speeches should be somewhere between 10-15 minutes long. (It may not seem like much time, but seven minutes is really the sweet spot. However, most speakers feel obliged to talk a bit longer than that.). A number of studies have been performed on how long one's attention span is so you should investigate it at your leisure. Of course, if the speaker is lecturing to bunch of elementary students, he might be pushing it at five minutes.

Start speeches with an acknowledgement of other speakers, if any, and then the crowd. Being humble is the key here because the speaker should feel privileged by the invitation to talk. If the crowd senses he is indeed obliging, they will tend to accept him much quicker.

Here's an example of the opening paragraph for a company vice-president who is speaking at a press conference at the onset of a major renovation project. The keynote speaker after him, by the way, is the governor.

Governor XYZ – it is a pleasure to have you at (place of business) today so you can see first hand how you and the state are assisting our plant in becoming a viable partner of the (region's) economy. I also want to thank our business colleagues from the surrounding area who join us today. And let me express my great appreciation and gratitude to our employees who are sharing in this important occasion.

Second, the speaker briefly introduces himself:

I am (name), (company's name) business group vice-president. It is an honor for me to provide a few comments during this special event.

This is a point where some speakers try to lighten the mood by including an anecdote, joke or a chance to poke fun at a defenseless person or themselves. Personally, this isn't my cup of tea; the speaker will need to make the decision of whether he or she wants a light moment here. The worse case scenario is that the speech writer interposes a joke and it fails miserably. Guess who gets the blame?

Next, and most significant, is the main body of the speech. Do not leave an audience guessing what the speaker is trying to say; immediately state the purpose for speaking.

Today we will officially begin construction on our $10 million (project name) which will allow us to efficiently produce widgets for many more years. It is our goal to complete the project by August 1, an aggressive timetable but one we are fully committed to achieving.

It could be taken for granted most people know why they are attending the press conference or meeting, but this is an opportunity to remind them of the day's activity. It also allows the speaker to stress the importance of his or her speech. In this case, there is an abundance of money being spent and scores of people affected by the project.

The next recommendation is what makes speeches stand out beyond others – it's adding a prop into the equation. For example, one day I had to testify in front of a committee of state senators and representatives about the importance of the aluminum industry. The night before, while drinking a can of soda, it donned on me to use the can as a prop. So, I took a thin-bladed hacksaw and severed the can about two thirds of the way down. It took four attempts (cans) to cut it just the way I wanted.

I then used a small amount of clear tape to piece it back together in a manner that no one could tell it was cut. During my speech, I talked about how our particular area produced one-third of the nation's aluminum supply and that if the aluminum industry disappeared there would be a detrimental affect on the entire state.

If you take a look at this aluminum can, it represents all of the aluminum produced in the United States. Right now this country makes about 1 million tons each year with most of it being utilized in the automotive, aerospace and other manufacturing processes. But what you may not realize is you are sitting in the middle of the hot bed of aluminum production – right here in our state. This is what we represent to the industry.

As I said this, I gently held the can up in the air and pulled it apart revealing the missing one-third. It was not meant to be melodramatic but to serve as a mental bookmark for those in the audience.

This part of the can symbolizes the amount of aluminum our region produces in relation to the entire country, about 33 percent. This is a huge amount and represents millions of dollars in salaries, thousands of indirect jobs, and millions more in regional purchases and taxes.

Now back to the company vice-president's speech.

If preferred, substitute a prop with a sample product your firm will produce with the new equipment. It can be positioned at the podium so that the speaker can point to it and describe it to the audience.

The (machine) we plan to install will provide us with the capability to continue producing high quality widgets, such as the one you see in front of me. These widgets are critical to our production process and are not readily available in the Midwest. To be blunt we would be forced to shut down the business if we couldn't make this (part).

Next, tell them exactly what you plan to do.

Starting immediately, we will dismantle (the old equipment) and replace it with a new and much more efficient system deemed to be among the best in the world. Furthermore, the new equipment will be safer to operate, and it will to allow our plant to continue being an upstanding environmental steward.

At this point, you are getting close to shutting down the speech.

Rest assured the company's commitment to invest $10 million in this capital improvement project is a clear indication we plan to be *here for many years to come. This is our home, and we're proud to be here.*

Offer thanks, once again, to everyone who helped make the project a reality.

Before closing, I want to say thank you to the staff at the (name of local economic develop group), especially the director who led the charge in helping us earn support for our project. And let me say thank you to our state economic development cabinet. They began working with us more than a year ago on our application to obtain a tax incentive package for this and another project planned in an adjacent department. I also want to recognize the governor, our elected leaders, and others who guided us down a path into state government.

Finally, I want to thank our employees. We have the best and most knowledgeable workers in the industry. Because of their continued efforts, we are able to remain a viable part of the local and state economies. Thank you all.

Obviously, there are all kinds of speeches – from persuasive to informative – so one size doesn't fit all. But all speeches have one thing in common: they are to written to convince your audience about a particular subject.

Delivering the Speech

To prepare someone for a speech, there are a few things to consider: What type of personality does the presenter have? Is he an introvert or extrovert? Will he get nervous? People get panicky for many reasons, but most of the time it's due to a fear of forgetting what they are supposed to say – losing their train of thought – even if they know the subject like the back of their hand. Some fear stumbling over words while others worry the audience will be bored or uninterested. Their anxiety is understandable, especially if the person doesn't give speeches very often. Who wants to come across discombobulated in front of an audience?

People who are selected to give speeches take vast comfort in knowing exactly what to say, which is why most depend on a prepared speech. However, while a prepared script may provide a sense of security, reading from a lengthy paper can be a snoozer for the audience. That's why note cards should be used instead of a script.

Glancing at notes forces the speaker to be more personable because his eye contact with the audience increases significantly. It also decreases the risk of a speaker losing his place while reading from a long-winded, prepared speech.

Let's imagine you are instructing someone on how to give a speech. Your first suggestion is to guarantee the speaker is in command of his subject – he knows what he's talking about. Most likely the person invited to give a speech will know about the topic so that shouldn't be a problem.

Here are some other ideas:
- Know the target audience prior to the speech. Don't plan to deliver a speech prepared for a group of CEOs when the audience will be high school students.
- Know if the group will be supportive of your discussion? If the speaker is a proponent of coal fired power generation stations and it turns out the audience is full of environmental activists vehemently opposed to pollution, it would be nice to know about it in advance.
- The speaker should become familiar with the surroundings – where the speech will take place. Will it be a classroom, town hall or auditorium? Don't let the speaker walk into a 1,000 seat lecture hall when he expects to be talking to a group of 50.

- The speaker shouldn't get wired on caffeine before the speech – no chugging coffee chased with a five-hour drink stimulant.
- Practice breathing before the speech.
- Above all, be conversational – relate to the audience.

PUBLIC SURVEYS CAN BE USEFUL – BUT BEWARE

Here's the best advice I can give to a company who's thinking about conducting a public survey to determine what people think about them: don't do it. Sorry to sound negative about this subject, but in my opinion this is not the most effective communication tool. Why? Because the results are normally worse than anticipated and most companies do very little with the results once they receive them. The bosses might study the findings and hold meetings to discuss them, but that's usually about the extent of their effectiveness.

Unlike employee surveys that are held every year or two to gauge worker satisfaction, public surveys are usually administered when the business is on the verge of a major project or they want public approval for something.

Keep in mind, too, that public surveys are expensive to conduct. Hiring an outside firm to develop the survey and then calling hundreds or thousands of people will cost in excess of $25,000 – and often twice or three times that much.

Still, some businesses covet the survey. I was once a colleague of a communicator whose business conducted public surveys at least every two to three years just to see what the public thought about them. The results were always the same: people were aware of their existence but the scores were never high enough to make management happy. So, they would spend thousands of dollars each year on advertising to promote how good of a company they were. Same story. Same results.

If the truth be known, most businesses who plan to conduct a survey already know how the results will turn out; they are just trying to get confirmation.

Doing it anyway

However, when the bosses want to conduct a public survey, come hell or high water, there's usually not much a communicator can do to prevent it from happening. So, let's take a look at surveying.

First, there needs to be a genuine reason to perform one. Let's presume a business is on the verge of requesting a government tax break, and it needs political approval. Knowing this might affect tax payers' bank accounts, the business needs to know if its idea will cause a public backlash.

So, it hires a firm (or does it unaided, which I don't recommend) to conduct a random telephone survey of city, county or state residents to gauge their reaction. What the company hopes to see as a result of the survey is that the public wouldn't mind paying a few extra tax dollars a year to support the industry. If the results come back in favor of the plan, then they are shared with politicians and general public. But if they are negative, then there's a lot of work that needs to be done to change the public's position. It's also unlikely that the company will voluntarily share these results with anyone.

Developing the Survey

Hiring an outside firm to administer the survey is preferential. Their organizers will write the questions, decide the order in which to ask them, and make the phone calls. The number of questions should be restricted to 15 or less – maybe up to 10 minutes on the phone with participants.

Surveys usually begin with a person introducing herself and the firm she is employed by. Next, the participant will be asked some type of "screening" questions to determine the participant's gender, age, or if he/she is a registered voter.

Then the meat of the survey begins. The caller will ask questions/statements to determine the awareness of the targeted business and whether the participant has a favorable impression of the operation. From there, the questions will be more pointed as the surveyor states the problem and whether the participant is willing to help solve it.

If the participant appears to be uninformed about the business or the stated problem, the surveyor will switch gears and try to inform them of what's happening. Once they do that, then they nonchalantly go back to the question again, figuring the participant will answer in the affirmative to help the business. Once the crux of the questioning is completed, the caller may ask a couple of closing questions that are easy to answer. Those might include household income or ethnic background.

It might take a few weeks for the surveyor to collect and report the results. Be wary of the surveyor at this point because they will appear overly optimistic about the company's chance to be successful. Why? Because they want your business.

Then comes the hard part; doing something with the results. That may include picking up on donations, advertisements and company tours if the results are undesirable. If they're good, then let the world know about it and go about your project plans.

Working with Journalists

Understanding their needs, for your sake

Chapter 8

BUILDING RELATIONSHIPS WITH JOURNALISTS

Journalists are a fickle species. They are analytical, courageous, egotistical, inquisitive, intelligent, outspoken, savvy, witty and sometimes open-minded. They are also emotional and opinionated just like the rest of us.

However, the difference between journalists and everyday folk is that they are expected to shield those feelings when reporting news – just give readers the facts, and they'll decide which way to lean. Maybe it's the mystique of yesteryear when journalists were deemed to be among the most unbiased people on the planet, and we expected them to shoot straight from the hip, without injecting their opinions.

But the line of demarcation between fact and opinionated news stories has certainly blurred these days – especially on television where "journalists" are more inclined to be superstars than they are to be true blue reporters. They are entertainers with an open microphone, howling under the guise of old school journalism credentials. Biased reporting has become so pervasive that we've become accustomed to it. So if you labor under the delusion that reporters are unbiased – well, forget about it.

And why is it necessary for the business communicator to understand this? Business communicators are in a position to work with journalists; therefore, they should recognize that honest reporting is not always a guarantee. With that being the case, the best one can do is to build a relationship with a journalist – to find out if he or she can be trusted to report the news factually and as unbiased as possible. After all, reporters will ultimately determine the type of publicity a business receives.

EVERYTHING IS ON THE RECORD

No matter how well communicators know their beat reporter they should use the utmost caution when invoking the alleged right of speaking "off the record". "Off the record" is supposed to be some kind of special covenant between a reporter and the person she is interviewing, basically saying the interviewee can talk off the record without having his or her comments printed in the newspaper or aired on television. The reporter is supposed to play along and only use the information to advance her investigation and not attribute it to interviewee.

That, my friends, is a big gamble. While some reporters can be trusted, it's best to NEVER talk off the record…and here's why:

Some reporters do not subscribe to the "off the record" presumption, and it can doom your career if you are not careful. Remember, reporters are paid to report news – and snare a significant story.

One former newspaper colleague of mine was vehemently opposed to talking off the record during an interview and would not promote the concept. If an interviewee said anything, it was on the record even if he or she said it was off the record. "They shouldn't tell me if they don't want it reported," my colleague said. And, he's right. If a journalist is told off the record by a city commissioner that the mayor was stealing funds, how could he not report it?

If, however, you are the overly trusting type and still believe that it's okay to speak "off the record", do yourself a favor and specifically say when you are "off" and "back on" the record.

WRITING PRESS RELEASES

Here's a delicate and comprehensive subject of concern for communicators – writing the legendary press release. There are differing views on when to write and distribute a press release and even more study on what should be included in the message.

Journalists depend on companies to inform them when something newsworthy is about to occur. They do this by calling reporters on the phone, sending emails or issuing press (or news) releases to announce what they consider to be a newsworthy event. This is a common approach that works fairly well.

Even so, a piece of paper with the words "PRESS RELEASE" blaring from the top does not guarantee instant status as an interesting story. People would be surprised at the number of "press releases" journalists receive that don't amount to a hill of beans. Many of them are written by sales managers hoping to gain some free publicity for their business. They might get away with it a time or two, but then they are branded news whores and relegated to the bottom of the heap. It's a guess, but probably about half of the press releases sent to journalists contain pertinent information while the rest are useless attempts at free public relations.

Journalists know the difference. As malicious as it sounds, when reporters receive an envelope that has the words "Press Release" pre-printed by a professional printer on the front, it's probably going into the trash. If they open a company's letter and get any hint of a sales pitch disguised as a "story", it will be eighty-sixed.

Here are some examples of press releases that will get trashed:
- A manufacturer awards $50 to a local school.
- A cleaning company makes its 500th service call (after being in business two years).
- A local bank plans an annual Halloween party.

On the other hand, here are some reasons to issue a press release:
- A manufacturer is getting ready to build a new facility that will result in more hiring.
- A company donates $25,000 to a local charity.
- A local factory sets a production record.

There's a subtle line between legitimate press releases and an organization's effort to get its name in print. So let's look at how to write a good press release.

Writing a newsworthy press release

Developing a respectable press release is a very simple task if one follows a few fundamental guidelines:

1. Include a captivating headline that succinctly announces the subject of the release. This is a critical component and may become the deciding factor on whether a journalist continues reading. For example, "Company XYZ will begin construction on $25 million expansion project."

2. Directly under the headline, write a one sentence subhead briefly summarizing the entire news release.

"Approximately 50 permanent jobs will be added to the workforce."

3. Ensure the body of the press release includes the "who, what, where, when, why and how." (See Chapter 2 about the 5Ws and H)

4. Include contact information so the journalist can call with any questions.

Most press releases are about four or five paragraphs in length and contain one or two quotes from the general manager or company president. Some releases stretch into a second page, but avoid going beyond that because it will challenge an editor's time and space. A decent reporter will contact the business for more information instead of printing the release as is.

Here is one way to structure a press release:

- Paragraph One: Write the name of the city, state and the date in bold font at the beginning of the first paragraph, followed by a couple of hyphens. Then start the release with something like this: "The Widget Company announces today it has received authorization to proceed with a $25 million expansion to its"...etc. This is the most important paragraph.
- Paragraph Two (manager's quote): "This is an exciting and monumental day for (Widget Company)," said (manager's name). "This expansion will allow our plant to be more competitive and sustainable"...etc. When using quotes, don't provide data or key pieces of information in them – save that for the next paragraph. Quotes should demonstrate some excitement for the project.
- Paragraph Three: "Construction on the new project will commence on...etc. with an expected completion date of...etc. As a result, the Widget Company expects to hire 50 more employees once the construction phase is completed and the facility becomes fully operational."
- Paragraph Four: "The project's design phase began more than a year ago"...etc. This is background information that may be used or cut by the newspaper.
- Paragraph Five (manager's quote): "I would like to commend the company and all of the employees who worked diligently to help us reach this point. Without their teamwork"...etc. Again, don't use data or fine details here.
- Paragraph Six: "The Widget Company first opened in (town name) more than 10 years ago and employs approximately 350." This paragraph tells a bit about the company that a

news outlet might use to fill space. It is important information but don't be dismayed to find they won't use it, especially if the business is occasionally mentioned in the newspaper or on the TV.

- Include company contact information. This is critical! There is nothing more annoying to a reporter than to have questions about a press release but nobody to ask.

The intention of this press release example is to get more interest from the media. If there happens to be a significant announcement and the contact does not receive a telephone call from a reporter requesting more details, then you are probably dealing with an apathetic journalist. At this point, you can, at least, hope it will be printed or broadcast correctly.

CREATING A Q & A LIST

One of the most helpful tools a communicator can create for management – and for himself – is a list of possible questions the media or other stakeholders might ask regarding a planned or unplanned event. Along with those questions are the answers.

This is aptly referred to as a Q & A List – a crutch a communicator can rely upon when the heat is turned up by journalists. It's not visually extravagant nor meant to be circulated; it's just a cheat sheet to be used for reference.

To develop such a list it's wise to put yourself in the shoes of an inquisitive journalist from a major newspaper, one in which you have no prior relationship. Local journalists covering a business may not ask the toughest questions because they have a sentimental investment in a corporate neighbor. But a journalist who doesn't know the company will feel free to punch you in the gut, so to speak.

So what kind of questions should a communicator ask himself? To answer that question let's assume a business is about to announce a 20 percent reduction in its workforce (We'll consider it a layoff).

Here's what I would want to know, if I were a journalist covering that particular business:
- Why are the layoffs necessary?
- Are these permanent job losses or will the workers eventually return?
- When did the company determine that a layoff is required?
- When was the last time you eliminated jobs?
- When will the employees lose their jobs?
- Is the company offering any type of incentives to senior employees to avoid layoffs?
- Are more layoffs possible?
- How did the company determine who to eliminate?
- Will other employees be expected to take on more work as a result of the layoffs?
- Is there anything that could have been done to avoid layoffs?
- Is the business restructuring?
- Is the customer base dwindling?
- Will the company offer retraining for employees being laid off?

Write the potential questions in bold font and the answers in normal font so that they can be distinguished from each other. If questioned by the media, don't read the answers verbatim; rather, practice them in advance so the answers sound natural. It might feel like overkill to prepare for so many questions, but it's actually a good idea to be over-prepared.

Here's a word of caution when being interviewed by journalists: some of them like to offer answers long with their questions. For example, a reporter might ask, "Why did you decide to lay off employees?" followed by: "Is it because your business is losing money? Did you lose customers? Is the corporation downsizing?"

In these situations, ignore his possible answers and stick to the script – the Q and A response. That way it's unlikely you or the interviewee will say something that management didn't approve beforehand. Danger lurks when one goes off script.

Employee Incentive Programs

The creative side of communication

Chapter 9

GIVING BACK TO YOUR EMPLOYEES

One of easiest and most sincere methods of recognizing a job well done is a simple "thank you" or a handshake. As unpretentious as it may appear, managers find it difficult to express appreciation to their workers because a) they do not take the time or b) they just don't want to. Getting bosses to provide employees with meaningful verbal recognition is sometimes like tugging on a stubborn mule.

Employees who perform their daily duties, as they are expected to do, should be praised for their personal contributions just as the high performers receive commendations for their work performance. In other words, the woman who comes into work every day and executes her job up to expectations and then goes home should occasionally be applauded for her efforts, in addition to any annual salary increase she might receive. What is wrong with people only doing their jobs?

Since the economy became sluggish, and with competition being more dynamic than ever, companies are starting to cut jobs – or at least not filling positions that were vacated by attrition. This means employees are not only expected to carry their workload but also some responsibilities of another position. It might be a bit presumptuous but this trend will likely continue and soon become the new normal for employee workloads.

Short of begging for more output from employees, managers must figure out a scheme to increase employee motivation and performance. The first step is to recognize their hard work and offer incentives to do more. Here are some programs and ideas to do that.

IMPLEMENTING A CLUB 100 PROGRAM

Let me introduce you to the greatest employee incentive program that a business can implement. It's called Club 100!

Club 100 is an initiative fashioned to reward workers for doing their regular duties and for going above and beyond their job description. That's right; employees get rewarded beyond remuneration just because they do their job. (At this point, one might speculate: "Instead of going to all this trouble, why not tell employees that if they don't get their required work finished then they will face the consequences? Well, a company can operate in that manner, the old school paradigm, but where's the fun in that?)

Here's how Club 100 works:

With Club 100, an employee receives intangible "points" whenever he or she accomplishes a certain work-related task. For example, if a lady completes mandatory training requirements for the year, she will receive 10 "points". The points are recorded on a specially designed card that she keeps with her.

The goal is to complete a list of activities during the calendar year (January 1 – December 31) and eventually reach 100 points. The more activities she completes, the more points she earns. The points themselves are redeemed for gift cards when she reaches certain point levels (25, 50, 75 and 100). If she does reach 100 points, she is then eligible to participate in a major drawing at the end of the year – hence, she would belong to Club 100. The major drawing includes several large prizes, including a brand new vehicle, vacation packages, televisions, $500 gift cards, cash, vacation days…etc.

The hidden agenda of Club 100 is to entice workers to complete the necessary "supposed to do" responsibilities of their job – such as training – and then progress beyond those customary duties by participating in activities they would otherwise exclude from their daily routine, like implementing cost savings ideas. Another bonus of Club 100, if it is used smartly, it can solve chronic issues such as rising absenteeism or health care costs.

Club 100 Point Opportunities

The beauty of Club 100 is that it's designed to fit a company's needs – managers decide how employees earn points and the amount of points tied to each opportunity. A list of qualifying point activities is provided to the workforce at the beginning of the year, and they are not changed. All employees receive the same list.

To give you an idea of how I set up a Club 100 program, here is a list of activities and assigned points employees could earn the first year we held Club 100. The illustration shows how we set up Club 100 in Year 4:

Attendance

A relentless problem our 500-employee business faced was unwarranted absenteeism. Our overall absentee rate hovered in the 11 percent category and was eating our lunch. When one employee missed work, his position would be backfilled – which required overtime. There were even some days during the year when attendance was so deficient, we were unable to operate critical equipment, and this amounted to thousands of dollars in lost production. So, we decided to add point opportunities to encourage better attendance:

- Perfect Attendance / Quarterly Q1:   5 points
- Perfect Attendance / Quarterly Q2:   5 points
- Perfect Attendance / Quarterly Q3:   5 points
- Perfect Attendance / Quarterly Q4:   5 points
- Perfect Attendance / Full Year : 10 points

After the first year, our attendance rate started improving because employees didn't want to miss out on Club 100 points. And here is a true story of how it worked to perfection: one of our departments had a secretary who missed several days a year by taking "personal days." You know – those days off that are neither sick days nor vacation days. When we created Club 100 points for perfect attendance, any days off other than vacation were counted against the employee, meaning he or she would not get perfect attendance.

When we explained to employees what qualified for perfect attendance, she learned that her "personal days" would keep her from getting the points. In the first five years of Club 100, she did not miss a day of work because she needed those points. Prior to that, she missed anywhere from 7-10 days a year.

To up the ante on attendance, the next year we eliminated the quarterly point opportunities and only gave points if the employee had perfect attendance for the entire year. At the same time, we increased the points for perfect attendance from 10 to 25.

Guess what? The number of employees who didn't miss one day during the year dramatically increased from 35 in year two to 185 the fourth year of Club 100. That, ladies and gentlemen, paid for the program all by itself.

But that's not all. Here are other point activities:

Health Point Opportunities

To positively affect employee health, we added point opportunities for proactive health care, including:

- Complete Health Risk Assessment: 10 points
- Complete Full Annual Physical :   5 points
- BMI (within weight range):   2 points
- Keeping Cholesterol Below 200:   2 points.
- Get a flu shot: 2 points
- Participate in Weight Watchers: 2 points
- Participate or join a health club: 2 points

Our motivation for this was due to the rising health care costs for our employees. The company's costs were increasing dramatically, and we had to respond in some hands-on manner. The number of employees completing their health risk assessment increased almost two-fold, and those employees completing a physical also increased tremendously.

And here's another story: As part of the physical, employees had to get a chest x-ray. In one instance, we had an employee who found out he had a serious form of lung cancer. But because it was caught early, he went through chemotherapy and was eventually deemed to be cancer free.

- Attend Wellness Presentations: 2 points
- Attend Wellness Presentations: 2 points
- Attend Wellness Presentations: 2 points

As you have seen by now, we wanted employees to recognize that their health is highly valued. Wellness presentations are held three or four times each year, and they consist of 30-45 minute programs featuring a local health professional talking about a particular subject. There were sessions held on dieting (eating right), mental health, dental and vision, just to name a few. When we added Club 100 points for attending these sessions, the number of participants climbed significantly.

And, here is another true story: We invited a local dermatologist to provide free skin cancer screenings for any employee who wanted it. Not only did dozens of employees take advantage of the screening, there were several identified as having spots on their skin with the characteristics of cancer. We had one lady that actually was diagnosed with skin cancer and had to undergo an operation.

- Donate Blood: 2 points
- Donate Blood: 2 points

The plant held blood drives at least twice a year (five hours a day) for the American Red Cross. The Red Cross would park their huge "Blood Mobile" bus in front of the administration building, and employees would donate if they had time.

After we implemented Club 100 and gave points associated with the blood drives, the number of donors increased by 30 percent the first year alone. In the second year, the number of blood drives doubled to four and the hours for donating increased to seven. At one of the blood drives during our second year of Club 100, we set a local record for the amount of blood donated in one drive. Employees also increased their donations from maybe once to three times a year – a significant triumph for the Red Cross. As a bonus, there were extra advantages for us from the public relations perspective because we promoted our blood drive successes in our annual report.

Department Point Opportunities
- Meet Department Key Performance Indicators: 10 points
- Exceed Department KPI by 10% or more: 10 points

There are no individual quotas for employees, but each department is expected to reach its respective production goals established at the beginning of the year. If they reach them, each Club 100 participant gets 10 points. If they exceed them, they could get 10 more. In other words, everyone in the department gets points or no one does.

Plant wide point opportunities
- Cost Savings Idea: 1-25 points possible. An employee can implement a cost-savings project and earn one point for every $1,000 he saves the company, capped at 25 points. To earn cost savings points, employees can propose a project and complete a one-page summary of the work they will do and the amount of money estimated to be saved. They submit the proposal to their department manager who then approves it for implementation. Once it's completed, our finance department determines the project's true value and then points are awarded.

Through the first three years of Club 100, our employees implemented projects that saved the plant just over $2 million!

Hello, Club 100! This part alone would pay for Club 100 the next 20-plus years!

Other point Opportunities

▪ About the same time Club 100 was being implemented our company was also incorporating a new Business Improvement (BI) initiative aimed at changing production processes to make them more efficient. The BI department then organized employee subcommittees to perform Kaizen improvement projects. If you're

Company Name

CLUB 100 (name)   EMPLOYEE_____ CLOCK_____

DATE	EVENT / ACTIVITY	POINTS	SIGNATURE
	Perfect Attendance / Full Year	20	(Supervisor)
	Meet Department KPI (Set by employee's department)	10	(Dept. Manager)
	Exceed Department KPI by 10% or more	5	(Dept. Manager)
	Cost Savings Idea – Must complete form (25 points max)	1-25	(Dept. Manager & Finance)
	Complete the Health Risk Assessment (Employee & Spouse)	5	(Wellness)
	Complete Full Annual Physical (Physical)	5	(Medical)
	Complete physical during scheduled time	5	(Medical)
	Participating on a Business Improvement Project	3	(Lead Black Belt)
	Participating on a Business Improvement Project	5	(Lead Black Belt)
	Plant 100 Consecutive Days without MTC	5	(Supervisor)
	Plant 100 Consecutive Days without MTC	5	(Supervisor)
	Plant 100 Consecutive Days without MTC	5	(Supervisor)
	45 Consecutive Days w/o MTC, LTII, First Aid by Dept.	5	(Supervisor)
	45 Consecutive Days w/o MTC, LTII, First Aid by Dept.	10	(Supervisor)
	Attend 1st Quarterly One-On-One meeting with your supervisor	3	(Supervisor)
	Attend 2nd Quarterly One-On-One meeting with your supervisor	3	(Supervisor)
	Attend 3rd Quarterly One-On-One meeting with your supervisor	3	(Supervisor)
	Attend 4th Quarterly One-On-One meeting with your supervisor	5	(Supervisor)

Company Name

CLUB 100 (name)   EMPLOYEE IS RESPONSBILE FOR HIS / HER CARD PROOF NEEDED FOR SIGNATURE

DATE	EVENT / ACTIVITY	POINTS	SIGNATURE
	Complete 1st TAKE 5 Book (must be turned in)	3	(Safety Rep.)
	Complete 2nd TAKE 5 Book (must be turned in)	4	(Safety Rep.)
	Complete 3rd TAKE 5 Book (must be turned in)	5	(Safety Rep.)
	Complete 4th TAKE 5 Book (must be turned in)	6	(Safety Rep.)
	Complete 5th TAKE 5 Book (must be turned in)	7	(Safety Rep.)
	Complete all OHS Mandatory Training	10	(Training Rep.)
	Body Mass Index (within weight range; see Medical)	2	(Medical)
	Keeping Cholesterol Below 200	2	(Medical)
	Attend 1st Plant Manager's Employee Presentation (plantwide)	3	(At Presentation)
	Attend 2nd Plant Manager's Employee Presentation (plantwide)	5	(At Presentation)
	Attend 3rd Plant Manager's Employee Presentation (plantwide)	7	(At Presentation)
	Donate Blood at Plant Blood Drive	3	(Wellness)
	Donate Blood at Plant Blood Drive	3	(Wellness)
	Mammogram or Prostate Examination or Colonoscopy	3	(Medical)
	Attend Wellness Presentation	2	(Wellness)
	Attend Wellness Presentation	2	(Wellness)
	Returning 2009 Club 100 Card to Administrator	3	(Administrator)
	Community Services	3	(HR)

not familiar with a Kaizen, it is a common business instrument used to moderate waste (costs) and make operations more efficient.

Because this was a fledging group of employees with a big task ahead of them, management decided to include Club 100 points for those employees who volunteered to be on Kaizen. (They could participate in up to three Kaizens a year, each worth five points.)

Safety Point Opportunities

To encourage employee safety, we provided points when the plant reached certain safety milestones, such as reaching 1 million hours without a lost time accident. Before Club 100, we customarily celebrated these milestones by purchasing lunches for all employees. It was a nice gesture and went over well for those attending. But because we were a 24-hour operation with a complex amount of swing shifts, the logistics for putting on one of these luncheons was absolutely terrible. If employees had to miss, for whatever reason, they expected to receive something in return. We found ourselves purchasing dozens of $15 gift cards from local restaurants for those unable to attend.

With Club 100, we dropped the practice like a hot potato and instituted the point system in the following manner.

- If the plant made it 100 consecutive days without a Medical Treatment Case or Lost time Accident (LTA): 5 points.
- If the plant made it another 100 consecutive days without a Medical Treatment Case or Lost time Accident: 5 points.
- If the plant made it a third 100 consecutive days without a Medical Treatment Case or Lost time Accident: 5 points.

Recording Points

The biggest concern we had with implementing Club 100 was the logistics around recording points and then proving an employee actually earned them. We developed 8.5 by 5.5 inch cards, printed on

60-pound paper. The cards were two-sided so all of the point opportunities would fit.

Our first inclination was for each department secretary to keep their employees' cards so they would not be lost. But since the emphasis of Club 100 was to entice employees to become more involved in the business, we came to the conclusion they should be responsible for their own cards.

Each time employees earned points, they were required to seek out the person heading up the particular activity and he or she signed off on the accomplishment. Put another way, if an employee finished his physical, the nurse had to sign the card, not his production supervisor.

Club 100 Reward System

To entice participation and continued support for the program, employees need to be rewarded for their efforts every so often (immediate gratification for a job well done). Otherwise, they might get bored with it and give up.

There are two ways to get rewarded in Club 100. First, each time an employee reaches a 25-point plateau he or she receives a gift card at whatever denomination you want to set. At our place of business, we gave employees a $25 Visa gift card when they hit 25 points; a $50 gift card at 50 points; $75 gift card at 75 points; and a $100 gift card when they maxed out at 100 points.

If you're trying to keep score, that means we give employees a total of $250 in gift cards if they make it to 100 points -- $25+$50+$75+$100=$250. Of course, if they hit the magical 100 points, they also become eligible for the end-of-the-year grand prize drawing.

Employees have the choice of getting their gift cards as they successfully move beyond each 25-point threshold, or they can wait until they make it to 100 points and get $250 all at once. (Waiting until they get all 100 points before cashing in will become more common because employees will wait until the end of the year so that they can use the money for the holidays.)

At this point, you might be wondering how much a program like this might cost. Well, if the business has 500 employees – and each one earned 100 points – you're looking at a possible $125,000 giveaway. Add in the cost of the new vehicle at $25,000 (plus the plant paid the taxes), and another $10,000 for other major prizes (trips, television, $500 gift cards…etc.), you're looking at $160,000-plus.

That may sound very expensive – that is until you look at the big picture. First of all, not every employee will participate – and not every participant will make it to 100 points. Second, think about all of the incentive "programs" your company now has in place and what it's like to administer them.

Club 100 can become an umbrella incentive program that can take the place of other incentive ideas that might be draining the company in other ways. Where I worked, we spent $75,000 annually on safety incentive prizes such as t-shirts, dinners, gift cards and other promotional items. We also paid a group of employees' overtime to serve on a committee to develop incentives. And that's not mentioning the countless amount of gift cards and such that they gave away randomly to employees for completing a specific task to earn a reward.

We were spending at least $175,000 a year in employee incentives and very few of them did anything to help us with employee morale or become a more efficient operation. Overall, we never spent more than $100,000.

Club 100 Grand Prize Drawing

As mentioned earlier, employees who reach the magical 100-point mark are eligible for the end-of-the-year grand prize drawing.

Sometime in late November, establish the date and time of the drawing – which should be in early January.

Make a big deal of it by sending personal invitations to eligible employees' homes congratulating them for their accomplishment and asking them to be at the drawing. It also serves a dual purpose by letting family members know about the gainful incentives occurring at work. It doesn't hurt, either, that employees can brag to their co-workers that they get to attend the drawing and have a chance to win a new vehicle.

To increase the excitement and inclusivity of the grand prize drawing, hire a caterer to serve eloquent hors d'oeurves and non-alcoholic drinks. Additionally, dress the place up with balloons, posters, and music so that there is a party atmosphere.

As for the drawing itself, there are several methods one can use to pull names for prizes. The most recognized, of course, is to give each employee a ticket with a number on it and then put it in a box along with the others. Someone then draws out the tickets from a box.

But here is another, more exciting idea: purchase cheap ping pong balls off the internet and write each person's name on a ball. Buy or borrow a round hopper to put the balls in for the drawing. On the day of the drawing, carefully place each ping pong ball, in alphabetical order, on an eight-foot table. Lay down masking tape (sticky side up) and put the balls on there to keep them from rolling around. When the employee arrives, he takes his ping pong ball off the tape and places it in the hopper.

In the presence of everybody in the room, the remaining ping pong balls of those who didn't make it to the drawing are taken off the table and placed in the hopper. Again, everything is to be performed in the presence of employees.

As noted earlier, our Club 100 grand prize drawing included a new vehicle that we bought at a local dealer. Since we were a unionized plant, it made sense to purchase American-made vehicles. So, we rotated the brand from year to year (i.e. Ford, GM, and Chrysler). Each August or September, we would purchase the new vehicle and park it in front of the administration building across from the main parking lot. We placed magnetic signs on the doors and a banner in front of it promoting Club 100. Within a matter of days, employees were swarming the vehicle and whetting their appetites.

To ensure that all Club 100 members have a chance to win the vehicle, the first ping pong ball removed at the drawing should be for the vehicle. However, to keep an air of excitement going, place the ping pong ball inside a small container (box) in a way nobody can see the name of the winner and hold it until all the remaining prizes are given away. When those are completed, pull the ball from the box for the grand prize winner.

Among the other prizes we gave away were:
- $2,500 and $1,000 vacation vouchers purchased from a reputable travel agency
- A $1,000 large screen television with a wall mount
- Popular MP3/video players
- Computer tablet
- Five $500 Visa gift cards
- Week vacation
- Birthday off
- Cash increments of $1,000, $500 and $100

It doesn't take large prizes at a grand prize drawing to make Club 100 successful. A lasting impression is made when employees are treated as honored guests for achieving 100 points.

ESTABLISHING A FIRST SNOW CONTEST

Those who live in an area that normally sees snowfall, here's an incentive idea: begin an annual First Snow Contest for employees. The concept of a First Snow Contest has been around for a long time;

many businesses, including radio and television stations, sponsor them every year. All people need to do is guess the day their area gets its first measurable snowfall – the operative word is "measureable", which is an inch. The person who picks the correct day or is closest to it wins a prize. If more than one person picks the same day, there's a drawing to select a winner. There is also an option of splitting the prize between contestants, which is up to them.

Registering contestants is a breeze. All anyone has to do is write his or her name and the guessed date on a pre-cut piece of paper and then drop it in a locked box. (They only receive one guess). Once the registration period is over, pick out the slips of paper and then record the names and dates of the guesses.

Type all the participants' names and the day they guessed on an 11 x 17 sheet of paper, laminate it, and then post it so everyone can see it. (It can also be made into a PDF and sent by email to all employees.)

There are two questions commonly asked about the contest: 1) who determines if the area records an inch of snow? 2) Where does the one-inch of snow have to fall?"

To answer the first question, choose a local television meteorologist (the closest TV station) to make the call – a person who is respected and trusted. Contact him or her around October 1 and ask if he will inform you of when the first one-inch snowfall falls at the TV station. Also request an "official" email when the snowfall occurs so that it can be forwarded to all employees.

As for the second question of where the snow must fall, it might be best to choose the TV station's property. Most businesses have employees scattered around their region – some just a mile away while others commute an hour or so. In a snowy region, some places might get a dusting while others get six inches. It's because of these variances that one central location should be deemed the target for a one-inch snowfall. And who better to do it than a local weatherman?

As the days slip away without snow – and there are always people who will guess early and late dates – mark through the names of those who had guessed too early. Don't completely black out the names because people enjoy teasing others for no longer being in the contest.

When snow is in the forecast, people who guessed dates falling within the forecast period are in the spotlight for the next few days. Once the "snow event" occurs and the meteorologist's confirmation is received, send the news out to everyone. It doesn't take long for the winner(s) to come forward.

By the way, if you are fortunate – or unfortunate – to receive considerable snowfall, consider having a contest on when a big pile of snow will melt.

ORGANIZING COMPANY PICNICS

Everybody loves a picnic, right? Then how about organizing one for employees as a way to show the company's appreciation for all of their hard work? They're fun, usually relaxing, and are meant for all ages.

Fundamentally speaking, there are two types of picnics: (1) something large-scale that might be held at an amusement park or (2) a charming get-together at an area lake or city or state park. Smaller picnics are much more conducive to personal interaction whereas amusement park picnics lend to employee disbursement. Either way, they both have some common denominators: employees and their family are invited; they are typically held on the weekend; they start around 10 a.m.; lunch is served for everyone; snacks and drinks are made available throughout the day; and there are games to participate in.

The first consideration for holding a company picnic is to find out how much money can be allocated to the event. The next is to find shelter or park availability. Let's take a look at the two types of picnics and what's involved in the planning process.

Old-fashioned Picnics

Old-fashioned picnics – the kind where there's an absolute reliance on human interaction – are what people often associate with a picnic: children scampering around having fun, people playing horseshoes and bingo, eating fried chicken and consuming ice cream. They seem to attract older employees because there's considerably less hustle than at an amusement park. Children seem to like them as well, as long as there's something to do.

Planning for this type of picnic should be started at least three months in advance – not counting reserving the picnic location (with a shelter) almost a year earlier. An ideal place will have a lake or some type of water feature to allow participants to swim or paddleboat.

At least 7-10 employee volunteers are needed to assist with the logistics, including: distributing tickets to employees, arranging caterers, purchasing prizes for contests, welcoming guests, giving out t-shirts or ball caps to attendees, directing games and tournaments, calling bingo, handing out prizes, and clean up.

At the first organization meeting, everyone should agree on their respective responsibility and then given the autonomy to get the job done. If somebody is handling caterers, let them do all the preparation – do not interfere with their work. When two people are assigned to purchase gifts for prizes, don't tell them what to buy – give them the final say.

And here is another idea for getting volunteers: pick a local high school organization – say the girls' golf team – and make a $500 donation to their team if they agree to serve lunch and snacks to everyone – and to clean the area. Have them arrive around 10:30 a.m. and introduce them to the crowd, then let them proceed with their hosting duties until 2:30. This is a win/win situation since it allows the high school organization to earn money to purchase items they may need.

Oh, and by the way, purchase something for each volunteer as a way of saying thanks, maybe a restaurant gift card.

Ticket Preparation

Begin the registration process at least one month in advance of the event. On the day of the picnic, give the employees an appropriate number of wrist bands he or she will use. This will distinguish the company's employees and their guests from others who may not be part of the event. Reinforce that the wrist band is required to enjoy lunch and refreshments.

Food

With an old-fashioned themed picnic or at an amusement park, it would be best to contract food services – maybe a local restaurant that will handle all the food and setups. The biggest challenge is making a judgment call on how much people will eat. As a precondition, most restaurants will want to have a fairly accurate count about a week before the event and then they will add extra food just in case. It's quite rare for a picnic to run out of food.

Games

The fun part of any picnic is the games. Since children and adults will attend, try incorporating activities for specific age groups. For example, have toy tractor rides for youngsters (have someone clock how fast they progress through an obstacle course) or find-the-money-in-a-haystack game (as a substitute for hay, use shredded documents). For the adults, the entertainment may consist of bingo, horseshoes, corn hole, volleyball and softball.

Award prizes for just about everything. With horseshoes and corn hole, maybe include a double elimination tournament – overseen by an employee volunteer – and give prizes for different age groups. Above all, just have fun!

Obviously, there will be a few obstacles along the way, but most of them will be easy to overcome – as long as the planning is thorough. Participants will have a wonderful time, and they will appreciate the organizers' and company's efforts.

Amusement Park Picnics

If the business has a younger workforce, say the average age is less than 40 years old, then an amusement park picnic might be the best choice. There are dozens of theme parks throughout the United States, and they all have one thing in common – there are plenty of rides and no one gets bored.

These types of picnics are easier to prepare because the park will provide support for games, food distribution and cleanup. The biggest problem the organizer will encounter occurs before the event takes place, which is taking care of ticket reservations and distribution. This can be a headache because some employees will take advantage of the company's hospitality by requesting tickets for friends and relatives; even worse, some may try to sell the tickets. If money is no problem, then let everybody pick up as many tickets as they want. Otherwise, establish some guidelines for how many tickets each employee can receive.

Even though employees will be scattered across the park, make sure to reserve a shelter of some kind to provide lunch and games (bingo, scavenger hunts, etc.) These activities, coupled with amusement park features, will keep employees busy from the time the park opens until it closes.

Employee Feedback

It's (kind of) a Two-Way Street

Chapter 10

How many employees out there would just love to tear into their boss about the awful job he or she is doing? Just the same, how many people are brave (and stupid) enough to actually do it? Most of us, at some time or another, want to address work concerns with our supervisors but hold back in fear of reprisal. And even if we wanted to complain or generate discussion about the simplest topics, there usually isn't an employee feedback mechanism to do so, other than the performance reviews or suggestion boxes.

Employee feedback is a worthy tool for an organization wishing to improve its operational performance. Feedback can lead to new discoveries, identification of faulty equipment, ideas for saving money, detection of a problem about to spiral out of control, or even be an outlet to let employees blow off a little steam. In essence, positive actions can derive from employee feedback, if it's properly administered.

There are numerous feedback mechanisms that can be implemented at work with the most common being employee surveys and face-to-face feedback – both of which are excellent ways of communicating. This chapter will explore those methods and others.

PUTTING TOGETHER A Q & A FORUM

Let's start with one of the best feedback mechanisms to incorporate – something I call the Question and Answer (Q&A) Forum. To briefly explain, the Q&A Forum is an internal link on a company's intranet that allows employees to submit an anonymous question or comment about their operation. They type their questions in an online form, click the submit button and then the comment is sent via email directly to the forum administrator. There's not a name associated with the email; the "sender" is called the Q&A Forum "guest". The question is then routed by the administrator to the proper person to answer. When the answer is received, the question and answer are both posted on the website.

To develop a Q & A Forum, assistance from someone in the Information Technology (IT) department will be necessary. He or she will need to make the site accessible to employees, develop a submission form, and then determine how to route the submission to the site administrator for review – probably through email. The IT department should arrange a login and password account for the administrator so that he or she can manage the site.

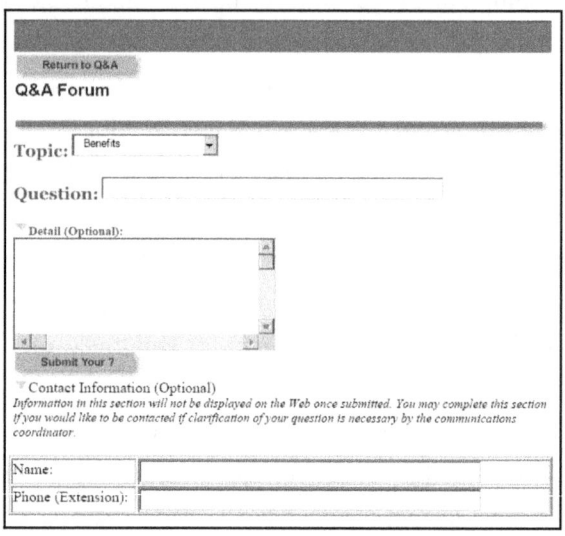

The forum should not be complicated. It will have a form where employees can type a question and then hit a submit button. Within seconds of hitting the submit button, the administrator (maybe the business communicator) will receive an email containing the question. It's important to note that the question ***should not*** be posted until it is edited and the answer is received.

Establish a dropdown list near the submission box so employees can choose the issue they want to address. Such topics might include benefits, work ideas, operations, safety, or management. (If "management" happens to be part of the list, then that's where most of the submissions will be channeled.)

Be forewarned that there will be nasty "questions" or comments that are not worthy of being posted. In fact, there's a good chance that 20-25 percent of them will be unprintable due to slanderous accusations, scatological language, or because of downright stupidity.

It really is quite amazing and entertaining to see what arrives by email. Thus, the administrator will need a thick skin to control the site – and some editing prowess.

Next to the submission form, post the questions and their answers so that employees can view them. No doubt the forum will become an instant hit with employees; they will check it every day for new submissions.

INCORPORATING EMPLOYEE SURVEYS

Employee surveys are utilized by companies hoping to find out how employees feel about their workplace – both the negative and positive aspects. Often called "engagement surveys", they are usually administered once every year or two and the results are measured against previous surveys.

Common topics for surveys include employee benefits (pay, health insurance, and retirement), business objectives, communication, employee incentive programs, and general employee satisfaction. Surveys will usually allow the respondent to rate their feelings about these particular subjects from low to high. A comment section will also be provided at the end of the survey

There are two common types of surveys: corporate and local. Corporate employee surveys are probably the easiest to administer because they arrive at the site already packaged and ready to be distributed. All that is needed from the communicator is to distribute, collect and return them to the agency overseeing the process. A few weeks later the business will receive the results.

Topics for these types of surveys usually run the gamut. Because they cover so many topics, the surveys can be painfully long – sometimes 70 or 80 questions – and take 20 minutes or so to complete. They usually list the same questions for every business around the globe – maybe just worded a bit different – so each site can be compared to the others.

The worst part about corporate surveys is they are never well-timed. Unlike surveys created in-house, there isn't much a communicator can do if one arrives shortly after a layoff, funding cutback or maybe when there's a problem with production processes. If this happens, a high probability exists that the results will be skewed to the worse.

For the survey administrator (communicator), there will be some pressure to achieve robust participation – at least 50 percent – to keep the corporate hounds at bay. With this being the case, they, in turn, will put pressure on employees to complete them. Some locations try to increase returns by offering a gift, say a water bottle or a pen, when an employee completes one.

Local Employee Surveys

Another type of survey is one created in house – by the communicator or management team. These are actually more relevant to the business because questions can be written specifically about the local operation, including shift schedules, remuneration, employee incentives or management philosophies. They are often much shorter, too.

When administering an internal survey, make sure of the following:

- Do not list more than 15-20 questions.
- Use mostly closed-ended questions: (For example: "Do you feel you have a safe work environment?" This way you can include answers ranging from "highly agree to highly disagree."
- Keep questions/comments in an affirmative light. (For example: Do not say, "My job requires me to work overtime every week." Turn it around and say: "I have an opportunity to work beyond my 40-hour workweek.")

- Dedicate an area on the survey where the participant can leave a comment (for management's use only.)

Don't Put the Results in a Filing Cabinet – Use Them!

Overall, employee surveys can be advantageous – but only if something is done with the results. A committee should review the results and determine action plans to address the most negative responses. For example, if the survey determines that a large majority of employees do not feel they are adequately applauded for the work they do, then the business might create an employee incentive model. It can take a team several weeks or months to design a plan.

Once the action plans are developed, it's time to publish the results – along with the action items – in a newsletter or other internal publication.

In summary, the most important aspect of employee surveys is to do something with the results – to create a plan to make improvements in the business. If that doesn't happen, employees will tend to opt out of the next survey.

www.ingramcontent.com/pod-product-compliance
Lightning Source LLC
Chambersburg PA
CBHW060853170526
45158CB00001B/340